Spiritual Hunger And Suffering

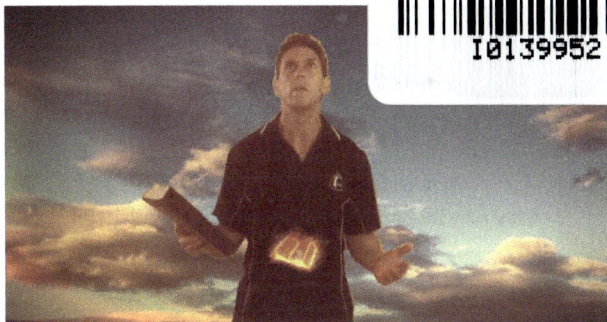

Why God Why?

Alistair J Pitman

Scripture quotations marked NLT are taken from the Holy Bible, New Living Translation, copyright © 1996, 2004 ,2007, 2013 by Tyndale Foundation. Used by permission of Tyndale House Publishers Inc., Carol Stream Illinois 60188. All rights reserved.

Scripture quotations marked NKJV are taken from the New King James Version Copyright © 1982 by Thomas Nelson, Inc. Used by permission. All rights reserved

Scripture quotations marked The Message are taken from The Message. Copyright © 1993, 1994, 1995, 1996, 2000, 2001, 2002. Used by permission of NavPress Publishing Group.

ISBN-10 0994361203 (Colour Printed Edition)
ISBN-13 978-0-9943612-0-2 (Colour Printed edition)

Acknowledgements:

This book in many ways is a journal of my family's walk over the last three and a half years. The contents of this book have flowed forth from countless hours spent in prayer seeking my heavenly Father. He has given me the strength, wisdom and insight to work through all that has come our way in this life. He is sovereign and His thoughts and His ways are truly higher than mine and I will continue to trust in Him regardless of the outcome.

To my now departed, loving and wonderful wife, Dorothy, of almost twenty one years - your strength, courage and commitment to follow God regardless of your pain and suffering, has truly set an example for many others, including myself, to follow. The ripples from your life will continue to vibrate throughout eternity. I will always love you Dorothy.

To my wonderful children, Kalani, Jayden and Kelby - you have been a wonderful source of strength and comfort to me. We have travelled this journey together and to see each of you grow in your faith even in the toughest of circumstances has been amazing.

To my family and Dorothy's family - the children and I are truly grateful for all the things that you have done for us. Without your practical help, love and support, both before and after Dorothy entered eternity; we would have struggled to move forward through this time of suffering.

To my close friends who have supported me over the last two and a half years - your wisdom, care, support and willingness to be there and listen, as well as offer advice, have in many ways contributed to the content of this book. Thank you for being there for me. I have been blessed, encouraged and strengthened because you took the time to care.

To Dorothy's friends, my friends, work colleagues, as well as all those who have followed our story through both email and Facebook updates - the support, care and feedback that you have given as I have sent out updates have been a constant source of encouragement.

Finally, thank you to Kathleen Nolan who took the time to proof read and edit this book for me to make sure it could be understood - I truly appreciate the effort and time you have put in.

Contents:

Preface: My Prayer For You

It is my prayer that the words within this book might literally burn within you as you read them. I pray that the words might inspire you and lead you into a deeper walk with God. Just as two men on the road to Emmaus had an encounter with the risen Lord and experienced His words burning within them, may you also experience words quickened in you by the Holy Spirit, burning deep within as you read about our journey. May they give you strength, comfort and understanding.

Luke 24:32 *And they said to one another, "Did not our hearts burn within us while He talked with us on the road, and while He opened the Scriptures to us?" (NKJV)*

It is the purpose of this book to show you how a person's spiritual hunger can either increase or decrease depending on how they handle suffering. Suffering is something that polarizes. For some, suffering causes the individual to seek God in a far greater way than ever before, and for others, suffering can cause them to turn their back on God and say, "How could a loving God let this happen to me?" This book is about my family and the choice we made to turn to God in the midst of suffering and who are now able to say, "How could we possibly have gone through what we have without a loving God to help support and guide us?"

This book outlines the journey we experienced both before and after my wife entered into eternity. It is hopefully a resource that people can look at, depending on what they have gone through or are going through, and find truths that we have learnt and held onto at various points in our journey that might help them. It looks at how God has been with us through it all and how He has helped us every step of the way, especially as we have chosen to follow Him in life, death and eternity. As we have faced difficulties and hardships along the way, God has opened His word up to us and revealed things to us that we were able to hold onto, that gave us the strength to carry on. God has been faithful and I know my faith has grown exponentially as I have turned to Him and relied upon Him. The wisdom and understanding that He has given us I pray will be of benefit to you, as you deal with whatever life brings your way.

May this book be a blessing to people who are suffering. May it be a blessing to people who are going through suffering with a loved one. May it be a blessing to those of you who have lost a loved one and may it be a blessing to all of you who desire to know God in a deeper and more personal way. May the words from this book burn within your heart, inspire you and motivate you to diligently seek God to an even greater depth than ever before.

Yours sincerely,

Alistair J Pitman

Chapter 1: Your Spiritual Hunger

A question that I love to ask people is: "How would you rank your level of spiritual hunger at this time?" If you had to give it a score between zero to ten (0-10) what would you give yourself? Zero meaning you have no spiritual hunger at all, through to ten, meaning your spiritual hunger and desire to know God is absolutely everything.

Psalm 42:1-2 *As the deer pants for the water brooks, so pants my soul for You, O God. My soul thirsts for God, for the living God. When shall I come and appear before God? (NKJV)*

I often picture a deer which has just escaped a lion. It has literally run for its life and now after escaping has found water. It desperately drinks the water. This is the image I love to have when I think of my soul panting for God. This to me reflects the ten. My spiritual hunger is such that I am desperate for God.

I remember a Year 12 Formal I attended for students a number of years ago. This function was in the city of Melbourne and when we arrived we were welcomed with non-alcoholic cocktails, followed by entrees, then a buffet and finally dessert. The cocktails were beautiful and I had two of those. The entrée consisted of satay sticks and they just kept on coming out and I just kept on eating. By the time we got to the buffet I was wondering how much more food they could give us and I was amazed when I saw what was laid out. They had platters of hot food, cold food, veggies, salads, steak, roast lamb, beef and much more! I piled the first plate high and then proceeded to work through it and then I went for seconds. After finishing about half of the second plate I was full. I mean really full! I had to leave food remaining on the plate.

From there things got even more interesting. Dessert was brought out and again it was buffet style with a huge variety. My eyes took it in but then because I was so full I couldn't stomach the thought of eating another thing and I was repulsed by the food. Even though there was plenty of food that I loved I had come to a point where I despised the food.

Proverbs 27:7 *A satisfied soul loathes the honeycomb, but to a hungry soul every bitter thing is sweet. (NKJV)*

This verse is very insightful. It has both natural and spiritual implications. In the natural, if we eat a lot of beautiful food such that we are full, no matter what is presented to us after that point we will despise it. We can't bear the thought of any more food, just as I experienced at the Year 12 Formal.

In the spiritual, if we satisfy our soul with the pleasures of this world it is possible we can become full and temporarily satisfied such that we despise the honeycomb that comes from God. What is it we fill our lives with day to day? Do we fill our lives with the pleasures of this world and the things of this life such that we have no room for the things of God? It is when we are spiritually hungry that no matter what God brings to us every bitter thing is sweet.

John 5:30 *"I can of Myself do nothing. As I hear, I judge; and My judgment is righteous, because I do not seek My own will but the will of the Father who sent Me." (NKJV)*

Jesus was one who was completely dependent upon the Father. For Him to state that He could do nothing of Himself is deeply thought provoking in terms of how I live my life. If Jesus could do nothing of Himself how much more true is this for me? Recognising my need for the Father causes a spiritual hunger to grow within me. We are in control of our appetite and we will ultimately hunger after that which we choose to feed on. What we feed on will be in direct proportion to our own personal need for God.

When you hunger after God and taste the honeycomb of hearing His words you want more. His word tastes so good that your hunger increases. When you feed yourself spiritually your appetite for the things of the Spirit continues to grow. When you don't feed yourself spiritually and you feed on that which this world has to offer your spiritual hunger decreases.

What is your spiritual hunger like? If you have no hunger for God you have no spiritual appetite. What have you filled yourself with? Is it the pleasures of this life? Are you so full that there is no room for the things of God? A question that I have asked in more recent times is what role can the suffering we experience play in all of this?

Chapter 2: Background To Our Suffering

The word 'Cancer' is something that can bring fear to the hearts of those who hear it for the first time. I can still remember when Dorothy told me for the first time. Dorothy had discovered a lump in her breast and had gone about having the initial tests done without letting me know what was happening. In her mind she didn't want the family or myself to worry unnecessarily until it was in fact determined what the lump was.

Dorothy and I had been married for twelve years when she was first diagnosed with breast cancer in August 2005. Kalani, our oldest, was six years old at the time, Jayden was four years old and Kelby had turned one a few months before. I was in Kelby's room changing a nappy and I still remember Dorothy coming in and saying, "I have cancer." I was floored to say the least and the initial reaction was one of shock, not knowing what to say or do, and the need to know whether she was going to live or die. The world as I knew it had changed and all I could do was hold her as she filled me in on the results and what they meant.

After the initial diagnosis Dorothy had a lumpectomy which didn't get the clear margins needed and then this had to be followed up with a mastectomy, that is, the complete removal of the breast affected. She also had to have two lymph nodes removed which we were informed could potentially be involved in the cancer going secondary if they weren't removed. After surgery Dorothy had to undergo chemotherapy and this was something we delayed for as long as possible so that we could follow a range of natural health remedies first.

The approach that we chose to take was to follow medical advice and embark on a range of natural therapies which included a change of diet. I supported Dorothy in all of this and the prognosis was good for Dorothy's chances of survival. For the first stage of breast cancer we were told that the likelihood of survival greater than five years was eighty percent of all patients diagnosed. Dorothy was declared cancer free almost two years later in 2007 and life started to return to some level of normality.

It had always been Dorothy's dream to travel the world and in light of these events we decided to make that dream happen. In October 2009 I took long service leave from teaching and together we travelled around the world for 105 days. We visited fourteen different countries and had one of our most special times as a family.

Two years later in October 2011 I took three more months of long service leave and during this time Dorothy and I had time together while the children still remained at school. It was a time for us to go out alone during the day and enjoy each other's company. This, as it turned out, was the last precious time that we had together alone before finding out the cancer had returned. It was indeed the calm before the storm!

In January 2012, on Australia day, Dorothy started to experience some serious headaches and went to the doctors seeking medical advice. At first basic medication was given to try and alleviate the problem but as the headaches persisted she was eventually referred to have a CT scan. On the day she had the scan I was on a three day Year 12 camp and it was during the second day of the camp that I received the worst text ever. I was having lunch with students and staff and I read a message that affected me in a way I had never experienced before. The text basically said, "I've just had the scan. They found a 5cm tumour in the brain. I could be in surgery tonight at St Vincent's Hospital. Call me."

As I read this message it was like a weight came upon my shoulders and my mind went cloudy. It was the same as having the flu and not being able to think clearly. I didn't know what to do and I couldn't get in touch with Dorothy straight away. I sat there like a stunned mullet and other staff started to ask me if I was all right and still in a daze I told them what had happened. I spoke to the Head of Secondary who was on the camp and he arranged to drive me home.

These physical symptoms were to stay with me for a period of three months as Dorothy and I came to terms with what lay before us. Dorothy ended up in surgery five days later, in order to have the brain tumour removed. It was determined shortly after this that the breast cancer had metastasized and gone secondary affecting both the brain and the liver. So began a whole new regime of doctors' appointments, radiation treatment and chemotherapy. Life as we knew it was changed forever and it is out of this experience that I wrote this book.

Chapter 3: Our World Changed Forever

The reason our world changed irrevocably with the news of the breast cancer going secondary was because we very quickly learnt that treatment was all about management of the cancer. Ideally that would involve finding the right treatment that would allow Dorothy's condition to stabilize so that she could live a relatively 'normal' life. A 'cure' for the cancer in terms of medical treatment did not exist but there were plenty of treatments out there that had been successful, enabling many patients to live for many years.

This is where I first became aware of how the place where we live is so important in determining the treatment that is available to us. For instance, if Dorothy and I had been living in a third world country she would not have been able to have surgery to remove the brain tumour nor would she have had access to all of the very expensive drugs that were out there.

I returned to work the following Monday after finding out on the Thursday that Dorothy had the brain tumour. I walked into morning briefing and I remember being asked how Dorothy was going and I had to respond to all of the staff present. I felt the looks of sorrow and sadness from every person present and it was too much for me. I didn't go back to briefing for the rest of the year! It was at this point that I started to withdraw and isolate myself from others, as every conversation would be of concern, making it difficult to focus on what I had to do.

It is important to note that the first time that Dorothy went through breast cancer I chose not to tell people at work what was going on with her health and most of our support came from the church. Work was my safe haven where I could focus on doing my job without distraction. There was no way that could happen this time because of my being on a camp when the information came out. However, as it turned out, work became the place where I found my closest friends who would support me right through until Dorothy left this life and beyond.

I was at this point experiencing the uncertainty of life. I had no idea of how life was going to unfold for Dorothy, myself and the children. My world was crashing down around me and for the first time in my life I was brought to a place where I could do nothing and everything going on around me was completely out of my control. It felt like a huge burden was resting upon my shoulders. The tension headaches made me think that I had something wrong with me too, and the only way I would find relief was to run and play golf.

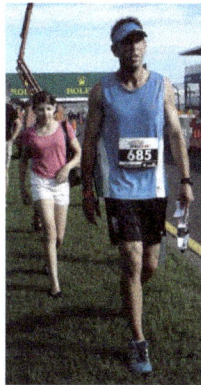

As I mentioned previously these physical symptoms continued for three months and only started to subside when it became apparent that Dorothy was going to live longer than I first expected. I must admit at the time I didn't think she was going to get past the brain tumour surgery because of the risks associated with it. My faith in God was somewhat rattled at this point and I began to ask a lot of the big questions. Why is this happening to us? Why would a loving God allow us to go through this? Why God, why?

Chapter 4: Why God Why?

This was the biggest question that confronted me during the three months after Dorothy was diagnosed with the brain tumour, as a result of secondary breast cancer. I was experiencing physical symptoms that I couldn't shake, and trying to make sense of everything with human reasoning was not accomplishing anything. Dorothy and I never believed that God gave her the cancer, but we believed He had allowed us to go through this experience for reasons known to Him.

Recognizing that God was in control and that God was sovereign in spite of our circumstances was something that helped us get a handle on things. We needed the peace of God in what was clearly a life threatening situation. God started to bring this about after a meeting I had with the chaplain at the school where all of my children were attending at the time. One of the key questions I was asked was, "How much have you let your children know about what is going on?" I revealed that we had mostly taken a positive approach and focused on what was being done to deal with Dorothy's health issues. One thing that came out of this conversation was that there was a family at the school whose mother had only told her children two weeks before she died that she had cancer and the children were now struggling as a result.

The reality of this situation hit home with me and later that day Dorothy and I had a really big conversation about the issue, while Jayden and Kelby were playing indoor soccer after school. It was during this conversation that I had a flow of thoughts and we received a word specifically for our situation that we were able to hold onto and share with our children as well. The word that we received and held onto was, "Dorothy is not going anywhere unless God says, 'Otherwise'."

It was this statement that allowed us to talk freely with each other, our children, our respective families and our friends. We could now talk openly about life and death. Previously it had been difficult to talk about death because it would seem to us and others that we were showing a lack of faith by not expecting Dorothy to be healed. Now I was able to say, "If God says 'Otherwise' what do you want your funeral to look like? Who would you like to take the service?" Dorothy and I discussed so many areas with each other because of the freedom this statement allowed us but it also meant we shared everything that was happening with the children. We didn't hide doctors' reports or medical results from them and we continually reinforced to them that mummy wasn't going anywhere unless God said 'Otherwise'.

Even though we had no answer to the question, "Why God, why?" we had a confidence in God that He was with us and He was in control.

Chapter 5: A New Resolve

It was in November 2012 that I remember spending the Melbourne Cup weekend at home, while Dorothy and the children visited her parents for the long weekend. I had students undertaking a Year 12 exam on the Monday so I still had to go into work and because our children had that day off Dorothy wanted to visit her family in Merino, four and a half hours away. I was okay with this and planned to spend the time in the most valuable way possible.

This long weekend was a defining period in my life where I spent four days seeking God and during that time resolved in my heart that no matter what, whether Dorothy lived or died, I was going to serve the Lord. I remember saying that I was going to seek Him like never before and if He wanted to wake me up during the night I would get up and seek Him regardless of the hour. Since that time I have sought Him in the early hours of the morning, as I have been woken up and there is no place that I would rather be, still to this very day!

One other significant thing had also happened just prior to this time (a few weeks earlier) and that was in relation to my diet. I had watched a small advertising clip that popped up on the internet (Beyond Diet) which challenged me about the way I was eating. It asked the question whether I was the type of person who went out for a run and then came home and proceeded to raid the kitchen for the rest of the evening. I responded with a resounding, "Yes!"

It then asked if I was the type of person who had sugar cravings and would try to satisfy the cravings with things like lollies and find it was only a short term fix, to be followed by more cravings a short time later. Once again I responded with a resounding, "Yes!"

As a result of this I signed up to their website and parted with $47! It was the best $47 I could ever have spent. I took their initial survey to determine the type of diet right for me and then started to chart what I ate for a period of three months. Within the first three days it became very obvious that I had a carbohydrate heavy diet and the balance needed to change. I decided to work on the balance of my diet, as well as cutting sugar out of my diet apart from fruit. I decided to give up soft drinks, cakes, ice-cream, lollies and a lot of processed foods and the results were staggering!

The first thing that occurred was I started losing weight. I went from 78 kilograms to 69 kilograms in a matter of six months and finally plateaued at 71 kilograms. I wasn't eating any less, I was just eating differently. The key thing here was I was still doing the same amount of exercise before and after I changed my diet. I ran 30-40 kilometres a week and completed a strength maintenance program four mornings a week. It was the change in what I ate that made the difference and shifting to a more balanced natural diet was highly beneficial. I had three meals a day with my only source of sugar coming from fruit shakes done in the blender each morning, which I would drink at morning tea and afternoon tea. I would have things like an apple, a banana, a couple of strawberries and some small pieces of pineapple mixed with water and blend them to make up two 600 millilitre bottles.

The most significant thing in all of this though, was that I went from needing 7-8 hours of sleep a night to 5-6 hours of sleep a night, and that extra time gained was spent diligently seeking God. Prior to this if I didn't get the sleep I needed I would get blood-shot eyes and become very tired and grumpy! I have now lived on 5-6 hours of sleep each night for over two years. A typical night for me might be going to bed at 10.30 pm, being woken up at 4.00 am and then spending time seeking God until 6.00 am. I would then go out and do my training program before coming back in and getting myself and the children organized for the day.

This change in diet coupled with a desire to get up and seek God whenever He woke me each morning became a part of my life from November 2012. It was as a result of this that I began to study the Bible and seek God like never before and God began to reveal truths to me that helped all of us as a family in terms of what we were facing.

Chapter 6: The Peace of God

Finding the peace of God in our situation was something that really came about as I started to diligently seek God. Questions like, "What is the peace of God?" and "How do you experience God's peace in the midst of suffering?", really started to challenge my thinking and what I've outlined below is the gradual unfolding of God's word to Dorothy and myself that kept us strong in spirit and mind, so that we were able to cope with everything that came our way during all of the treatment. It is my hope that what God revealed to us during this point in time may also encourage those of you who are going through trying circumstances. Some passages of Scripture in relation to God's peace include the following:

Philippians 4:7 *And the peace of God which surpasses all understanding, will guard your hearts and minds through Christ Jesus. (NKJV)*

Colossians 3:15 *And let the peace of God rule in your heart, to which you were also called in one body; and be thankful. (NKJV)*

Isaiah 26:3 *You will keep him in perfect peace, whose mind is stayed on you, because he trusts in you. (NKJV)*

Proverbs 3:5-6 *Trust in the Lord with all your heart, and lean not on your own understanding. In all your ways acknowledge Him and He shall direct your path. (NKJV)*

From these passages I made the following summary: to be in a place of perfect peace, that is, a place where I am experiencing the peace of God, I need to have my mind focused upon Him and trust in Him completely. To trust in God means to place your confidence in God. We don't have to understand why we are going through something to experience God's peace because it surpasses all understanding. The peace of God will guard your heart and mind through Christ Jesus.

Consider some of the tough things that people can be confronted with in this life: losing a job, poor health, loved ones facing battles with cancer, accidental deaths, car accidents, work place injuries, etc. The list is endless and the question must be asked how can we still experience God's peace in the midst of such circumstances?

The **first** thing I came to realise was that we often don't see the big picture as God sees it. We see things out of our limited frame of reference and we have questions. Consider Job who was a man in the Bible who faced extreme hardship and suffering. Job was an upright and blameless man who loved God and to look at what he had to go through in terms of suffering puts what our family has had to go through into perspective. It's easy for us to read the book of Job and see how God allowed Satan to do certain things to Job, including great personal loss, but Job had no idea of what was going on or why. Did God orchestrate what happened to Job? No, but He did allow it to happen. Job's friends offer a lot of advice and theories to help explain things but they lacked understanding and were no help to him and were in fact rebuked by God.

Consider healing. Why do some people get healed and others don't? Again we don't often see the big picture as God does. Does healing fit within God's overall plan at that moment in time? Would my relationship with God and Dorothy's relationship with God have become as strong as it did if everything had been going well and Dorothy had been completely well? Does God allow us to go through some of these things to redirect us to what really matters and perhaps change our focus? It has been everything that we went through that caused us to turn to God. I have learnt to be secure in the fact that God is doing things, or allowing things to happen, according to His plans and purposes. I can feel safe in that knowledge.

The **second** thing I came to realise is that we are to cast our burdens upon the Lord and we are also to cast our care upon Him for He cares for us.

Psalm 55:22 *Cast your burden on the Lord, and He shall sustain you; He shall never permit the righteous to be moved. (NKJV)*

1 Peter 5:6-7 *Therefore humble yourselves under the mighty hand of God, that He may exalt you in due time, casting all your care upon Him, for He cares for you. (NKJV)*

The word burden refers to those things which come our way in this life, that is, one's lot or portion in life (due to nature, what is given). In other words we are to cast or throw at the Lord those things that have come our way by nature, lot or portion. Many of the tough things that come our way in life fall into this category and this is what God wants us to do. Why? It is a part of coming to that place where we can experience the peace of God. With Dorothy we recognized that the breast cancer came our way and it was not for any reason or fault of our own, it just was, and we were instructed to throw that burden on the Lord. We didn't believe God orchestrated it, although He allowed it to happen.

We are also to cast all of our care upon Him. To cast your care upon the Lord in this context means taking all that matters to us, what might be causing anxiety, stress, worry, feelings, etc. and placing them upon God. There is a distinct difference between casting your burdens on the Lord and casting your care upon the Lord. One involves taking the burden and throwing it on the Lord whereas the other involves taking those things that matter to us and placing them upon the Lord. It's like saying, "Here Lord take this care, take this matter. I am putting it on You because I can't deal with it right now."

What is the peace of God? Based on a word study I arrived at the following definitions:
peace (Greek) - the tranquil state of a soul assured of its salvation through Christ, and so fearing nothing from God and content with its earthly lot, of whatsoever sort that is.
peace (Hebrew) - peace, quiet, tranquility, contentment, friendship with God

In summary: To me the peace of God is the peaceful, calm and quiet state of the heart and mind that is assured of salvation through Christ, fearing nothing from God and content with trusting in God no matter what one's earthly lot might be.

In **Matthew 7:24-27** there is the powerful illustration about how a person, who listens to God's teaching and follows it, is wise like a person who builds on solid rock, and a person who listens to God's teaching, but doesn't obey it, is foolish like a person who builds a house on sand. Whether a person is foolish or wise does not come to light until the storms of life come against them. The person who hasn't been obedient has no foundation to stand on when the storms of life come and their lives will crash and the peace of God won't be experienced by them. The person who is able to stand through the storms of life is someone who has not only listened to God's word but obeyed it. Even though they are in the midst of a storm they stand strong and firm. They continue to obey God and they experience the peace of God.

Dorothy and I experienced together a storm of life. It was when we recognised that God held the future in His hands and all we had to do was trust in Him, obey and keep a hold of His word to us that the peace of God came upon us. The peace of God surpasses (exceeds) all understanding.

I know God allowed His peace to settle in our hearts and that helped override our understanding. The peace of God replaced our uncertainty about the future. To fear nothing from God and to be content with trusting in Him, no matter what our earthly lot might be, kept us strong. We had security and safety in God and it was this mindset that helped rule our heart and mind, and everything that flowed out in terms of thoughts, passions, desires, appetites, affections, purposes and endeavours.

Even now, after everything that has happened, I still don't know what lies ahead for my family but the one thing I do know is that God holds our future in His hands and that is enough for the children and me. We will trust Him no matter what. We are confident that God knows what He is doing and He will accomplish His plans and purposes through all of this. We accept that God's ways and God's thoughts are higher than our ways and our thoughts and that He might choose to do things differently to what we might hope for or expect. Our confidence is in the Lord and our peace is truly found in Him.

Isaiah 55:9 *For as the heavens are higher than the earth, So are My ways higher than your ways, And My thoughts than your thoughts. (NKJV)*

Chapter 7: He Understands

Experiencing the reality of God's peace in our lives, even in the midst of suffering, was and continues to be a source of comfort and strength for us. The fact, however, that Jesus understands what we are going through makes a big difference. This was a truth that we received in early 2013.

Hebrews 4:14-16 *So then, since we have a great High Priest who has entered heaven, Jesus the Son of God, let us hold firmly to what we believe. This High Priest of ours understands our weaknesses, for he faced all of the same testings we do, yet he did not sin. So let us come boldly to the throne of our gracious God. There we will receive his mercy, and we will find grace to help us when we need it most. (NLT)*

As I studied the word 'understand' I found that it meant to feel sympathy, to have been affected with the same feeling as another, to feel and have compassion for another. This immediately started me thinking about how Jesus had been affected in similar ways to both Dorothy and I. The word 'weaknesses' refers to the body and soul. In relation to the body it is speaking about its natural weaknesses and frailty, and in relation to the soul it is referring to bearing trials and troubles in our mind. Jesus was tested in the realm of the body and of the soul. He faced tests in relation to how He would think and how He would behave in the midst of suffering just like us.

In the Garden of Gethsemane Jesus cried out to the Father.

Mark 14:35 *And He said, "Abba, Father, all things are possible for You. Take this cup away from Me; nevertheless, not what I will, but what You will." (NKJV)*

Jesus knew what He was about to face. In His humanity He asked if it was possible to let this cup pass from Him, but His resolve was still to do the will of the Father. The anguish that Jesus was feeling at this time was so great that He was ministered to by an angel and His sweat became like great drops of blood falling to the ground (**Luke 22:43**).

Both Dorothy and I said, "Lord we have learnt so much through suffering. You have brought us closer to Yourself, You have brought us closer to each other and You have brought us closer as a family. If possible, please let this cup pass from us Lord. We know that You can and You are able to heal but ultimately You choose whether to heal on this side of eternity or the other side of eternity. Please heal Dorothy from her cancer on this side, nevertheless, not our will be done Lord but Yours." Does Jesus understand our mental anguish of the soul? I think He does.

In the lead up to His death, Jesus was whipped, had a crown of thorns placed on His head and was then crucified on a cross. The pain that He went through was horrific and He went through it all for us. Dorothy suffered ongoing pain for over two years, none greater than in the final week of her life. Does Jesus understand our physical pain? I think He does.

In His final moments on the cross Jesus experienced the worst pain imaginable. To feel God the Father abandon Him as He became the sacrifice for our sin was something He had never experienced before. He asked a big question of the Father.

Mt 27:46 *"My God, My God why have you forsaken Me?" (NKJV)*

Jesus knew what it meant to ask, "Why?" He experienced the Father leaving Him to die on the cross. One thing we don't have to experience, if we choose to accept what Jesus did for us, is God leaving and forsaking us. The price Jesus paid for us was laying down His life so that we can enter into a relationship with the Father. So often we question and ask, "How could a loving God do this to us?" or "How could He do that to them?" As I have said previously, perhaps the more appropriate question is, "How could we go through what we are without a loving God to help us?" Does Jesus understand our questions? He truly does!

John 3:16-17 *For God so loved the world that He gave His only begotten Son, that whoever believes in Him should not perish but have everlasting life. For God did not send His Son into the world to condemn the world, but that the world through Him might be saved. (NKJV)*

Dorothy and I were able to draw so much comfort from the fact that we serve a God who understands. We mightn't receive the answers to our questions, or see God work in the way we hoped He would, but He does see the big picture and we have to trust that He knows exactly what He is doing.

Chapter 8: No Harm Comes To The Godly

Dorothy and I chose to live our life together for God regardless of the cancer that was causing issues with both her liver and brain. Our resolve was that no matter what, we would serve the Lord. As we searched for wisdom from the Bible in relation to our situation, we came across the following verse.

Proverbs 12:21 *No harm comes to the godly, but the wicked have their fill of trouble. (NLT)*

I struggled with this verse when I first read it and asked God for an explanation. I immediately thought of how many godly people have experienced harm and in fact even death and this verse seemed untrue, especially if it is looked at in light of our time here on earth. Consider the following: Paul the apostle was a godly man who contributed a significant portion of the New Testament as we know it today, yet he was executed for his faith. John the Baptist was a godly man who came in the spirit of Elijah and he was beheaded. Peter who denied Jesus three times was another godly man executed upside down on a cross. Jesus, the Son of God, was killed on a cross and He was completely innocent. Dorothy was a godly woman and she had her body filled with cancer and from all outward appearances seemed to be experiencing harm. Others have lost loved ones who were godly people, tragically through car accidents, work place accidents, acts of terrorism and many other things too numerous to mention. It was, however, as I looked at this verse in light of eternity that I gained a fresh perspective.

It is sobering to note that we are here for such a brief time on earth compared to the other side of death where you live in eternity. The Bible likens our time on earth to being like a mist or a vapour.

James 4:14 *How do you know what your life will be like tomorrow? Your life is like the morning fog - it's here a little while, then it's gone. (NLT)*

This life is preparation for the next. The choices we make now ultimately determine where we will spend eternity.

2 Corinthians 5:1-5 *For we know that when this earthly tent we live in is taken down (that is, when we die and leave this earthly body), we will have a house in heaven, an eternal body made for us by God Himself and not by human hands. We grow weary in our present bodies and we long to put on our heavenly bodies like new clothing. For we will put on heavenly bodies; we will not be spirits without bodies. While we live in these earthly bodies we groan and sigh, but it's not that we want to die and get rid of these bodies that clothe us. Rather we want to put on our new bodies so that these dying bodies will be swallowed up by life. God Himself has prepared us for this, and as a guarantee He has given us His Holy Spirit. (NLT)*

Our relationship with God on earth determines our relationship with Him in eternity. As I have begun to fully comprehend that there is more to life than just my time on earth here and now, and as I have realised that this life is preparation for eternity, I have begun to live and think differently.

Death is not the end of me. Death is not my termination, but my transition into eternity. There are eternal consequences to everything I do on earth. Every act of my life has the potential to strike a chord that will vibrate in eternity.

Hebrews 13:14 *For this world is not our permanent home; we are looking forward to a home yet to come. (NLT)*

As I meditated upon these verses another one came to mind which really helped me.

Matthew 10:27-28 *What I tell you in the darkness, shout abroad when daybreak comes. What I whisper in your ear, shout from the housetops for all to hear! Don't be afraid of those who want to kill your body; they cannot touch your soul. Fear only God, who can* *destroy both soul and body in hell. (NLT)*

The way in which I viewed 'harm' radically changed as a result of this verse. I am not to be afraid of someone who can kill my body; they cannot touch my soul. But rather I am to fear Him (God) who is able to destroy both my body and soul in hell. True harm is when you end up in hell, but when you look at all the people I mentioned above, true harm has not come to them because they are now in heaven where they have a new 'house', an eternal body, made by God Himself. A godly man such as Paul was killed for his faith, but no harm came to him in the sense that life with God in eternity could not be taken from him. Peter, John the Baptist, Dorothy and all other godly people who have died are on the other side of death in eternity with Jesus who rose again. No wonder Paul said, "to live *is* Christ, and to die *is* gain" (**Philippians 1:21**).

1 Corinthians 2:9 *But as it is written: Eye has not seen, nor ear heard, nor have entered into the heart of man the things which God has prepared for those who love Him. (NKJV)*

Both Dorothy and I believed that, as we allowed God to work through us each and every day, the things that He accomplished through us would strike chords that would vibrate through eternity in a powerful way. If God is able to minister to just one person through us because of our story, which in turn leads them to minister to someone else, then our experience and what we have gone through has been worthwhile.

We continued to respond in obedience to the leading of the Holy Spirit because we believed, along with our children, that Dorothy was not going anywhere unless God said 'Otherwise'. We truly held onto this truth that no harm comes to the godly. We may lose our lives but the reality is that the time we spend on this earth is nothing compared to eternity. Because of Dorothy's cancer and the suffering she had to endure, her life struck a chord in many people's lives and those chords will continue to vibrate through eternity.

As a result of this study we came to the point of viewing our life together as not being about us but rather all about God. When we gave our testimony we shared about how Jesus, the hero of our story, 'rescued' us even in the midst of what was a desperate situation. He drew us to Himself in a whole new way and we experienced the reality of His presence in a greater measure than ever before. We learnt to see ourselves as vessels that God filled daily so that what He had filled us with could be poured out to bless the lives of others. We wanted God to be able to flow freely through us. We wanted rivers of living water to flow forth from our family into the lives of others in spite of all Dorothy was enduring.

**1 Corinthians 10:*13* *No temptation or test that comes your way is beyond the course of what others have had to face. All you need to remember is God will never let you down; He'll never let you be pushed past your limit; He'll always be there to help you come through it. (The Message)*

This verse was a source of encouragement to us because it helped us cope with everything Dorothy had to go through. In light of all the passages above both Dorothy and I lived with the assurance that God was with us and ultimately no harm would come to her!

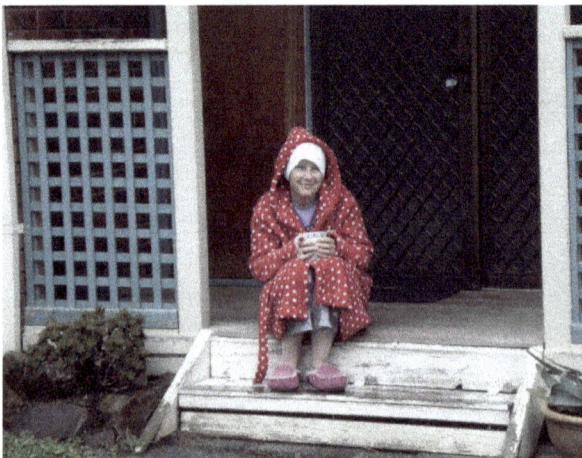

Chapter 9: In The Darkness

It was during the early months of 2013 that a verse in Isaiah was passed onto me by a close friend at work. Both Dorothy and I drew a lot of encouragement from this as we studied and meditated upon what it meant and how it related to our situation.

Isaiah 45:3 *I will give you the treasures of darkness and hidden riches of secret places, that you may know that I, the Lord, who call you by your name, am the God of Israel. (NKJV)*

Isaiah 45:3 *And I will give you treasures hidden in the darkness - secret riches. I will do this so you may know that I am the LORD, the God of Israel, the one who calls you by name. (NLT)*

Isaiah 45:3 *I will give you the* <u>*treasures*</u> *hidden in the* <u>*darkness*</u> *and hidden riches of secret places. I will do this so you may know that I am the Lord, the God of Israel, the one who calls you by name. (NKJV & NLT combined)*

The reason we found this to be an extremely encouraging passage of Scripture was because we had been going through a time of darkness as a family. The word 'darkness' here refers to times of <u>uncertainty</u>, <u>confusion</u>, a <u>desperate situation.</u> To know that God gives you treasure in these times as you seek Him is very comforting.

God in fact gave to us new insight and freedom through this time of darkness. God gave us treasures, necessary supplies, an armoury, a magazine of weapons, so that we might truly know that He is God. He called us by name in the midst of darkness and we knew that He was with us through it all. For me personally the term secret place is very significant. The secret place is the place where I spend my time with God

Matthew 6:6 *But you, when you pray, go into your room, and when*

you have shut your door, pray to your Father who is in the secret place; and your Father who sees in secret will reward you openly. (NKJV)

God revealed to both Dorothy and I His hidden riches in the secret place during this period of uncertainty, confusion and desperate situation. My secret place is truly when I meet with Him in the early hours of the morning. There is no place that I would rather be! This fits in beautifully with the following verse which says:

Psalm 27:8 *My heart has heard you say, "Come and talk with me." And my heart responds, "LORD, I am coming." (NLT)*

No matter how great the darkness, I meet with Him in the secret place because He calls me by name. My God calls me by name to come and talk with Him. This is a strategic place, a well camouflaged location from which I can operate.

Isaiah 50:4-5 *Morning by morning He <u>wakens</u> me and opens my <u>understanding</u> to His will. The Sovereign Lord has spoken to me and I have <u>listened</u>. I have not rebelled or turned away.*

God wakens me each day at various times in the early hours of the morning. It is then that He opens my understanding to His will. Ever since November 2012, when God started waking me up morning by morning, it has literally been like God saying, "Alistair, come talk with Me" and the response of my heart has been, "Lord I am coming, Lord I am there."

I remember a close friend asking me how long did I think God was going to continue doing this and at the time I had no idea, but I believe God has since revealed to me that as long as my heart is willing and I desire to spend time with Him, He will keep on waking me up. When I wake up, for example at 3.00 am it is not like I feel sluggish and lack energy to get up and pray but rather it is like I'm woken, bolt upright, out of sleep and I just want to seek Him. There is no place I would rather be and I love these early hours of the morning.

Isaiah 50:10 *If you are walking in* <u>*darkness*</u> (confusion, uncertainty, a desperate situation) *without a ray of light, trust in the Lord and rely on your God. (NLT)*

Dorothy and I walked in darkness for a little over two years. This was a place where there was <u>uncertainty</u>, <u>confusion</u> and a time of <u>desperate situations</u>. We didn't know what the future held. We didn't know what each new medical report would bring and half the time we didn't know what those reports really meant. Sometimes I saw small glimpses of where God was taking us, but God was leading my family through this darkness day by day and it was for our protection.

To know the future clearly and know where God was taking us was not what He wanted for us, because it would cause us to stumble. If we knew as a family in advance everything that we were going to go through right back in August 2005 we would not have been able to cope. Rather as we chose to live according to God's quickened, living word day by day He gave us the strength that we needed. The darkness caused us to turn to Him and trust in Him like never before.

Psalm 119:103-105 *How sweet your words taste to me; they are sweeter than honey. Your commandments give me understanding; no wonder I hate every false way of life. Your word is a lamp to guide my feet and a light for my path. (NLT)*

Although at times I struggled being in the darkness, God continued to wake me morning by morning. He has been speaking to me throughout and I have been listening. It has been absolutely vital that I do this day by day because His word to me each day has been a <u>lamp to my feet</u> and a <u>light to my path</u>. My understanding of this Psalm took on a whole new reality as I linked God's word to my experience each day. God's word each day was enough to see a few steps ahead and give us the strength to keep moving forward in the darkness.

Even though it was dark all around, God was still giving us the light to see what was going on in our immediate vicinity, as well as the next few steps ahead. We learnt not to try and light our own fires or sparks to see where we were going but rather we chose to allow God's word unfold to us day by day.

I learnt not to try and do things in my own strength. God was unfolding His plans and His purposes to us bit by bit. He was giving us that which we needed in order to be able to do His will. My family had to endure a lot with Dorothy's life constantly hanging in the balance but we chose to continue obeying His instructions. This life is all about Him and all that mattered was being obedient to Him. The darkness that surrounded us caused us to trust in God. We knew that He was able to see through the darkness, and He would continue to unfold His plans, His purposes and His will in His time.

Both Dorothy and I believed that as we took the treasures and hidden riches that God revealed to us through the darkness and in the secret place, and as we began to impart and declare them daily to all we came in contact with, He would bless and touch the lives of others. There is always hope in God in the midst of darkness and no harm can come to us when we look at things in light of eternity.

The darkness was something that we were going through together as a family and we chose to put our trust in God as a family. We continued to hang onto the word that Dorothy was not going anywhere unless God said 'Otherwise'. Dorothy would be with us until God chose to take her home to Himself. Could God still move in our time of darkness? Absolutely, but things don't always happen in the way we would like them to. All I know is God sees the big picture and He knows what His plans and purposes are and to let the peace of God rule in our hearts was critical for us to stay strong in this storm of life.

As a side note to all of this I remember going out for a run one night during this period of darkness, to process and work through in my mind where everything was at. As I began the run I started to have a flow of thoughts in relation to my love for God and for Dorothy. I focused on how love is a decision and it is a choice that we make. Love is an act of your will.

From here my flow of thoughts went to our marriage vows where I reflected on the fact that in marrying Dorothy I had vowed to have and to hold her for better or for worse, for richer or poorer, in sickness or in health, to love and to cherish until death us do part. It seemed, as I thought about this, that this vow was being fulfilled on the down side at that moment in time. We were going through some of the most difficult circumstances we had ever gone through (for worse). Financially we were okay but it was in sickness that we were working through life at that time.

My thoughts then shifted from Dorothy to God. I was thinking of how I often say, "I love You Lord." and then I thought, "Do I really, because I don't feel anything?" It was towards the end of the run that I put these thoughts out there and all of a sudden God clicked everything together. When I am saying, "I love You Lord", I am communicating that I love God because of a choice that I have made. I have determined in my heart, regardless of circumstances to love Him. It is an act of my will, a decision of my heart (not based on feelings) that communicates to God that I love Him. That choice or decision in turn completely affects everything I do. I love God and when He says, "Come talk to me", I respond with, "I am coming

Lord" because I genuinely want to be with Him (**Psalm 27:8** NLT).

It was as I declared this to God at the end of my run when I was at walking pace that I had a 'mountain top' experience. God enveloped me with His presence as I declared, "I love You Lord", and I literally felt the Holy Spirit permeating every part of my being. He touched my spirit, soul and body. My body was literally tingling all over and I had hair standing on end all over my body for 20-30 seconds. I sensed God in an amazingly, powerful way. Given that I am the type of person who in the past has had the sensitivity of a brick, the subtlety of a sledge hammer and the emotional climate of the North Pole, for me to have this experience was quite significant and I knew beyond a shadow of a doubt that I loved God and that He was with Dorothy and myself every step of the way! I now also know that, as I hear from God and do according to that which is in His heart and mind, He is helping me to have a little more sensitivity, subtlety and enabling me to express my emotions a little more than before. God was with us in and through the darkness and I knew this in a whole new way.

It was also very significant that after this experience I was able to thank God for taking us through this time of darkness. Why God, why? Maybe, just maybe, God allowed us to go through this so He could draw us into a deeper level of relationship with Himself and in turn touch the lives of others.

Chapter 10: Drawing Strength From God's Word

My suffering has been good for me because it has shown me what is important in this life. It has taught me to pay attention to God and His word like never before.

Psalm 119:71-72 *My suffering was good for me, for it taught me to pay attention to Your decrees. Your instructions are more valuable to me than millions in gold or silver. (NLT)*

I have allowed God to turn my eyes from worthless things to Him and His revealed, living, quickened word. When faced with the reality of death my priorities in life changed radically. The possessions of this life become a hollow pursuit, especially when the one you love and share everything with is potentially not going to be there anymore

Psalm 119:37 *Turn my eyes from worthless things, and give me life through Your word. (NLT)*

God is my place of refuge and He really is all I want in life. I have found that He has kept me in perfect peace as I have stayed my mind on Him and invariably it is only when my mind starts to focus on the circumstances of life that I start to spiral downhill in my way of thinking.

Psalm 142:5 *Then I pray to you, O LORD. I say, "You are my place of refuge. You are all I really want in life." (NLT)*

By His divine power He has given me everything I need to live a godly life. I am coming to know Him in greater measure and by the receiving of His great and precious promises I am able to share of His divine nature.

2 Peter 1:3-4 *By His divine power, God has given us everything we need for living a godly life. We have received all of this by coming to*

know Him, the one who called us to Himself by means of His glory and excellence. And because of His glory and excellence, He has given us great and precious promises. These are the promises that enable you to share His divine nature and escape the world's corruption caused by human desires. (NLT)

It has been encouraging to know that we are not alone in our suffering, and that there are Christian brothers and sisters all over the world who are going through suffering and we can be there for each other. And after suffering He will restore, support and strengthen us and I know that He is already doing that now for my family.

I Peter 5:8-10 *Stay alert! Watch out for your great enemy, the devil. He prowls around like a roaring lion, looking for someone to devour. Stand firm against him, and be strong in your faith. Remember that your Christian brothers and sisters all over the world are going through the same suffering you are. In His kindness God called you to share in His eternal glory by means of Christ Jesus. So after you have suffered a little while, He will restore, support and strengthen you and he will place you on a firm foundation. (NLT)*

May these verses be meaningful to those of you who can relate to, and identify with, what we have been going through.

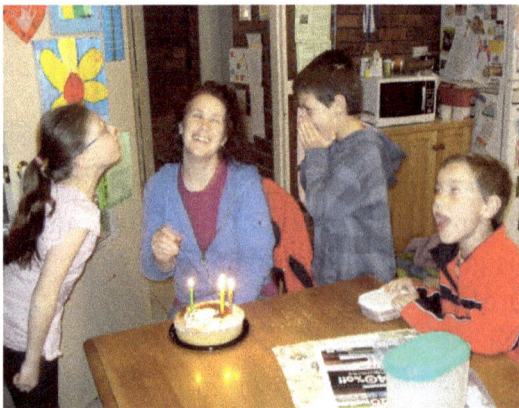

Chapter 11: Handling Bad News

In late October 2013 we received medical test results that hit us, initially, pretty hard as a family. Things had been relatively stable for ten months or so with the treatment that Dorothy was on at the time and then all of a sudden a tumour in the liver had increased from 3 centimetres to 6 centimetres and lesions in the brain had grown in number and size. Dorothy initially struggled with the news and did not want to speak to anyone for the next couple of days while she was processing the information for herself and what it meant for us as a family.

We chose to let the children know these results as well and their reaction when we told them was noticeably different for each child. Jayden was vocal and expressed his concern to us. Kalani was quiet and knew the significance of what was being said and how things would change in terms of treatment. Kelby just changed the topic which was his way of dealing with it. He was internalising the news, not wanting to think about it.

I, like Dorothy, was initially shaken with the news when we were told, because I was not expecting the changes to be quite so significantly different from previous tests. I personally was very flat and discouraged that night wondering, "What now Lord?" My head became cloudy once more as stress and worry started to affect my thoughts.

However, the next morning God woke me up early and put a few verses on my heart which I have written below.

Psalm 112:7 *They do not fear bad news; they confidently trust the Lord to comfort them. (NLT)*

Psalm 27:14 *Wait on the Lord: Be of good courage, And He shall strengthen your heart; Wait, I say, on the Lord! (NKJV)*

Psalm 55:22 *Cast your burden on the Lord, And He shall sustain you; He shall never permit the righteous to be moved. (NKJV)*

It was at this point in time that I believe God communicated to us not to be afraid or fearful of what was coming our way. I was not to fear or be afraid of the bad news that had come our way. We were to continue to confidently trust in the Lord that He would care for us as a family. It was a time where we as a family needed to wait on the Lord and He would strengthen us. No matter what was to happen God would look after us all. God right then in the midst of our situation strengthened our attitude of heart and mind and we chose to trust in Him regardless of our circumstances, and continued to cast all our burdens upon Him, knowing that He would sustain us.

As I drove to work this same morning I was listening to a song by Chris Tomlin called 'Sovereign', and some words of the song really touched me. The song speaks about God being sovereign and how He is with us in the calm, with us in the storm and with us in the dark. As I listened to the words of this song I had an awareness of God's presence resting upon me. I decided at this point to pray out loud and as I did this God spoke to me directly in a very firm and powerful way. The words flowed from within and I had a real sense that God was making a declaration over my life and my family.

The main words that flowed forth were:
"In this coming period of time know that I am with you My son, I am with Dorothy, I am with your children and I am with your family. I am with you!"

These words reverberated within my whole being because I felt they were communicated in such a firm and powerful way. I was brought to tears and this was definitely something new, given I'm not really one who is in touch with my emotional side! I knew without a shadow of a doubt that God was right there with us as we were to go through everything coming our way.

The second way in which God spoke to us was through a passage of Scripture sent to me by a key leader in the school where I was teaching. It related to the Book of Daniel and three men who were being thrown into the fiery furnace and how they were able to declare their allegiance to God regardless of the outcome. This was something very significant that we chose to hold onto as a family.

I looked at the passage and the attitude of heart of Shadrach, Meshach, and Abed-Nego was amazing, given the situation they were facing.

Dan 3:16-18 *Shadrach, Meshach, and Abed-Nego answered and said to the king, "O Nebuchadnezzar, we have no need to answer you in this matter. If that is the case, our God whom we serve is able to deliver us from the burning fiery furnace, and He will deliver us from your hand, O king. But if not, let it be known to you, O king, that we do not serve your gods, nor will we worship the gold image which you have set up." (NKJV)*

The word God had given us in the past and the one we were still holding onto was that Dorothy was not going anywhere unless God said 'Otherwise'. The attitude of heart of the three men, in the passage above, is what we as a family wanted to have in our situation. We knew our God could and was able to heal Dorothy but if He chose to say 'Otherwise' we would still serve the Lord. Our allegiance was to Him regardless of the outcome. His ways, His plans and His purposes are far above our thoughts and ways and all we could do was trust Him. All of our lives are in His hands.

The final way in which God helped us in this situation was through a daily reading from a close friend at work. The reading they passed onto me contained some words written by Felipe and Mary Barreda who were twentieth century martyrs.

Faith is not expecting that the Lord will miraculously give us whatever we ask or feeling security we will not be killed and that everything will turn out as we want. We learned that faith is putting ourselves in His hands whatever happens good or bad. He will help us somehow.

As I read this I thought of Stephen in the Book of Acts who just before He was stoned saw Jesus at the right hand of the Father and his face shone like an angel. He was stoned and he died, but God was right there with Him. I also thought of the 'Footprints' poem where in the times of trouble it was God who was right there carrying a person in the difficult times where there was only one set of footprints in the sand.

In our situation we had hope that God could and was able to heal Dorothy, but we also recognised that if He said 'Otherwise' then He would continue to be right there with our family. Regardless of the outcome God was with us and we knew that He was touching us day by day and giving us the necessary strength to live our lives.

Chapter 12: Changing Schools

Two months later in December 2013 we found ourselves in a position where we had to continue to trust in God and there was no way we could lean on our own understanding or wisdom. The medical results continued to get worse and Dorothy was informed that she would no longer be able to drive. She had experienced numbness in her left hand and lips while driving and this was of considerable concern. Not only was she potentially putting her life in danger, but also the lives of the children, as well as other people on the road.

Our prayer in all of this is written below and flowed from a study of **Proverbs 3:5-6** *PTV (Pitman Translated Version)*

"Lord at this time we are to place our confidence in You. You will make us feel safe and secure in this desperate time. We can only experience this as we rely upon You. We will trust in You out of our heart and not our intellect. We will lean on You for support and not on our thoughts or comprehension. You ultimately are the one who can be trusted and leaned upon not our own thoughts or ideas. God is directing and will continue to direct our paths and no matter what, we will rely upon Him."

One of the things that became a very real reality, as a result of the medical findings, was we had to look at the possibility of Jayden and Kelby shifting schools. It would have been a 'big ask' to rely on my mother to help us indefinitely with getting the children to school and that wouldn't be fair on her. The next day after the appointment I spoke to administration staff, at the school where I was teaching, about the possibility of Jayden and Kelby coming to my school and there was a place in Year 7 for Jayden, however, I would have to wait to find out for Kelby. I spoke to the principal about the possibility of the children coming and he was extremely supportive. I also inquired at another school close to home and there were spots available there also. Issues arose however about possible after school care.

By the end of the day I was leaning towards the school where I taught but there were still questions that I had. What would be best for our children? What would be best for us as a family? Where was I going to get most of my support from? What direction was God going to take my family? If I left the school to teach somewhere else would the boys have to shift again? All of these questions were very real questions that needed to be answered. We needed to be prepared since Dorothy had to stop driving.

After tea that night, Dorothy and I spoke with the children about the latest medical results and the possibility of shifting school, and the initial reactions were dismay and sadness. Kalani was prepared to do whatever it took to stay at the school where she was and committed herself to catching public transport. The boys had just done orientation days for their classes for the following year so it was hard for them. We had brought up a month or so earlier that there might be a possibility of this happening, so although they were upset it wasn't a total shock. Jayden was visibly upset because he didn't want to leave his friends but Kelby took it in his stride. Over the course of the next two days, being a weekend, we found out the Orientation day for Grade 4 was on the Tuesday and I already knew it was the Year 7 orientation day on the Tuesday and Wednesday.

The fact that I had already had conversations with administration staff and the principal on the Friday, to make sure it could happen for Jayden going into Year 7, was helpful, and then on the Monday I had a chat with the Head of Primary to see what the possibility was for Kelby. There was one thing that really stood out as significant. When I went and spoke to the Head of Primary and he asked which year level Kelby would go into, I said Grade 4 and he informed me there was only one spot left and he had just been about to offer it to a family, but the spot was now Kelby's. Again this reinforced to me that God was moving in all this. Another spot opened up later in the day for the other student who was going to be offered the place but we didn't know that at the time. I was given a spot for Kelby at that moment in time which was extremely supportive and a real confirmation, given I had been praying for open doors.

The next day on the way to school (Orientation day), I chatted with the boys about how as Christians we bear the name of the Lord Jesus Christ. We might face suffering and persecution because we bear His name, but also the name of Jesus can be honoured because of the way we live. I then spoke about how both of them bear my name and how because of that they might suffer some flack because they are my children. Other students might talk to them nastily about me and I talked about how they could respond. The first thing that I showed them in terms of responding is that they can say what others might say is not true and we love our dad. I then brought out how if the nastiness persists they could go to the coordinator or another teacher.

I then went on to talk to them about how it is important that they can also bring honour to our family name and to God by the way they live and conduct themselves. Teachers might sometimes have higher expectations of them because they are a staff member's child. All I want for them is to bring honour to God and to our family by the way they live. They can bring honour to our family like Kelby did with the soccer best and fairest award and like Jayden did with his academic awards in Grade 6. The boys responded positively to this word and I knew God was preparing them.

When I arrived at school we went over to the Year 7 meeting area and a colleague was fantastic. She grabbed her son and introduced Jayden to him and to all his friends. This was a real ice breaker and then another teacher's son came over and introduced himself as well. Jayden pretty much paired up with him for the day because they were in the same class. He went on to have a fantastic day as a result of all this. The students that Jayden was to be placed with

47

were what was really important to me given he was the most upset about leaving his friends and I believe God's hand was in all of this to help Jayden fit in quickly.

I then took Kelby over to the Grade 4 area and seeing him at the end of the line, quite tall and staring out and looking over the class with a boy near to him bursting into tears made it really hard for me as a dad, given I was the one putting him in this situation. He then walked off with the class and in my heart I said, "Lord please let this go well." At recess I got feedback that Kelby had settled in well and finished his work quickly and interacted with other students in a friendly way. He wasn't having any issues and his teacher said he was coping well. Jayden's teacher told me that Jayden was happy to engage and answer questions. He was with boys he met at the start of the day and Jayden commented himself at recess on how friendly everyone was and how he felt like he had been at Plenty Valley for years. The teachers and students were great!

At lunch time Kelby finished up and he was buzzing. He came along to the barbeque put on for the Year 7s and after asking if he was allowed to have a sausage, which he was, he was pretty happy and Jayden was happy to come up and chat about how the day was going. Playing dodge ball in the gym was an absolute highlight for both of them and Kelby thought all of his Christmases had come at once when I said he could go join in.

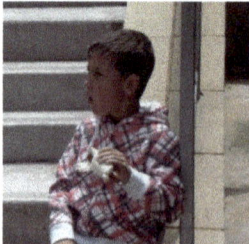

At the end of the day they got to meet other children who had parents on staff and they played. All in all they had a fantastic day! An encouraging thing that Jayden said to me at the end of the day was, "I love it at this school dad and I can't wait to start next year." The best thing of all that he said to me was, "You know Dad, I'm proud to bear your name!" Kelby thought his teacher was great and he enjoyed making new friends even though he couldn't remember most of the names of the other boys.

We then went on to a Maths/Science staff breakup where the boys continued to have a fantastic time with the other boys whom they had met after school. If they weren't sure before this they certainly were afterwards. I know God had His hand in all of this and the boys were going to be fine. God also gave Dorothy a verse that confirmed to her we were doing the right thing and she could see when the boys got home how excited they were, as could Kalani.

Psalm 126:3-6 *Yes the Lord has done amazing things for us! What joy? Restore our fortune, Lord as streams renew the desert. Those who plant in tears will harvest with shouts of joy. They weep as they go to plant their seed but they sing as they return with harvest. (NLT)*

This verse was really confirmation for Dorothy that God had done exactly this with our boys. They had a real joy about going to Plenty Valley, far more than what I ever expected or dreamed of, and all of this took place in four days from the time we told them about Dorothy's results and their having to shift schools. Was God with us? I know He was at that time and He still is today.

Chapter 13: Looking Past Personal Pain

The following passage is one that both Dorothy and I really started to apply to our lives as her health continued to deteriorate.

Matthew 14:13-14 *When Jesus heard it, He departed there by boat to a deserted place by Himself. But when the multitudes heard it, they followed Him on foot from the cities. And when Jesus went out He saw a great multitude; and He was moved with compassion for them, and healed their sick. (NKJV)*

The context for this passage is John the Baptist has just been beheaded by Herod because he promised the daughter of Herodias to give her whatever she asked because her dancing had pleased Him. Jesus when He heard that John had been beheaded was clearly grieving as He withdrew and went off by Himself. However, when He sees the multitude has followed Him, He is filled with compassion for them and healed their sick.

Even in a time of personal pain Jesus looked past what He was going through and saw the needs of those around Him. This in many ways was the place where God had been bringing Dorothy and myself to. Even though we were going through a time of increasing suffering because of the cancer progressing we became far more aware of the needs of those around us. We were more interested in giving of what we had received through our experience rather than wallowing in depression, fear of the unknown and anxiety.

Something a friend said to me that I remembered during this time was in relation to his teaching career. He expressed how he wanted to finish his career well before retiring. Both Dorothy and I held onto this mindset in a spiritual context where we wanted to run this race of life well and we definitely wanted to finish well. It wasn't how we started that counted but it was how we crossed the finish line.

2 Timothy 4:7 *I have fought the good fight, I have finished the race, I have kept the faith. (NLT)*

This is something that both Dorothy and I took on board because we were constantly being confronted with the other side of eternity. Dorothy in relation to this race of life had always wanted to impart to our children a godly heritage. She had wanted to see our children having made their own decisions to serve God and follow Him and it was and continues to be amazing to see their growth in faith through all of this. Dorothy had also wanted her life to be an example to others, including both friends and family. She had wanted people to see in her life, even in the midst of suffering, that her relationship with God was what was most important to her. She wanted God to be able to work through her to help others even in the midst of all of her treatment.

Dorothy was a godly woman who cared more about others than her own well-being and you would never hear her complain about what she was going through or the hardship that had come her way. Dorothy wanted the joy that she had found in God in the midst of suffering to be evident, to give others hope that no matter what comes your way God is the One in control and He still intimately cares for you.

Something a friend, from church and basketball, shared with me was *"If we are to accept God's miracles we also need to be able to accept God's mysteries."* This was something that really rang true with us at this time. Some things we go through are a mystery but we trust in God regardless. Do we wish what we have had to go through in terms of living with cancer on anyone else - No way! But do we wish people could learn from our experience in terms of what we received along the way - Definitely! God through all of this has changed our lives irrevocably forever.

Dorothy and I continued to run the race that God had set before us. Although we didn't know what awaited us, we continued to run the race with joy and continued in the ministry which we had received. We continued to share the good things He was doing in our life together even in the midst of suffering. The reason we were able to continue to run the race with joy was because we knew that He was with us every step of the way and we were living in obedience to Him.

1 Corinthians 9:24 *Do you not know that those who run in a race all run, but one receives the prize? Run in such a way that you may obtain it. (NKJV)*

Acts 20:22-24 *And see, now I go bound in the spirit to Jerusalem, not knowing the things that will happen to me there, except that the Holy Spirit testifies in every city, saying that chains and tribulations await me. But none of these things move me; nor do I count my life dear to myself, so that I may finish my race with joy, and the ministry which I received from the Lord Jesus, to testify the gospel of the grace of God.*

Faith comes by hearing, and hearing by the word of God. The word that we had received and held onto continued to sustain us. We were persuaded, convinced and absolutely inwardly certain that Dorothy was not going anywhere unless God said 'Otherwise.' He is the One in control and He is the One who releases in us the divine enablement to be able to do what He wants us to do. It was this word that sustained us and gave us the mind set to be able to share with our children and others all that we were going through.

Psalm 39:4-5 *Lord, remind me how brief my time on earth will be. Remind me that my days are numbered - how fleeting my life is. You have made my life no longer than the width of my hand. My entire life is just a moment to You; at best each of us is - but a breath. (NLT)*

Psalm 31:5 *I've put my life in your hands. You won't drop me, you'll never let me down. (The Message)*

All of our days are considered brief or short in the context of eternity and all that Dorothy went through gave us a heightened awareness of this truth. With this knowledge we had been given a different perspective. It wasn't suffering that brought us closer to God, but rather it was our response to suffering that brought us closer to God.

One of the greatest joys in my life is to hear God's spoken word to me and to do accordingly, and my joy is made complete when I in turn have the opportunity to share that word with others and they in turn are inspired and motivated to walk in a greater depth of relationship with God. To see others grow and move into a closer relationship with God is an amazing thing to behold.

Chapter 14: Our Lives Are In His Hands

March 2014 was a very tough time for our family. Dorothy's blood test results continued to get progressively worse and as a result of the treatment Dorothy's quality of life deteriorated.

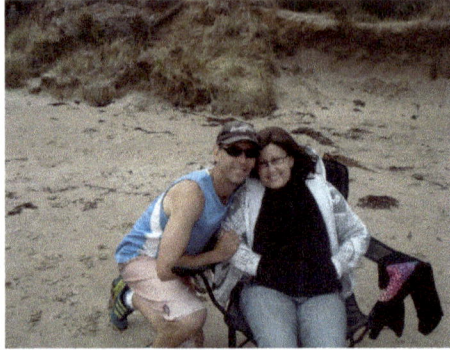

The cancer marker relating to the liver had gone from 89 in January, to 248 in February and then to over 400 (normal <39) in March. The marker relating to the brain had gone from 154 in January, to 415 in February and then to over 700 (normal <2.5) in March.

The tumours were continuing to increase in size and this was confirmed by the Oncologist through a physical examination in Dorothy's liver region. Dorothy could feel the liver pressing on her abdomen and this caused her quite a large amount of discomfort on a daily basis. The main concern with the blood test in March related to the enzyme counts in the blood relating to the liver. For example, one of the enzymes is meant to be less than 51 for a normal person and Dorothy's count had gone from 93 to 251, to 926, to just over 1300 and this had all been since December 2013. There are four different enzymes in the blood test related to the liver and all of them increased significantly. These enzyme counts indicated how well Dorothy's liver was getting rid of toxins in her body, and the answer was quite clearly not very well!

Dorothy had a very bad reaction to the chemotherapy during this time and she experienced swelling throughout her body. Her knees were hurting and she got to the point where she could barely walk. The reaction she experienced was one doctors had not seen before, but given it was another type of chemotherapy drug and her liver was having difficulty getting rid of toxins from her body, the cocktail mix of drugs was enough to send Dorothy to hospital so that the pain levels could be treated with morphine.

This reinforced to me that the treatment itself was now contributing to Dorothy's pain and suffering, as well as a reduction in her quality of life. There comes a point where treatment does more harm than good and the treatment was threatening her life rather than extending it. It was extremely difficult to reach a decision to stop the treatment. To stop treatment meant that Dorothy's condition would continue to worsen and she would move from this life to the next. How do you prepare for that? How do you prepare your children for that? The alternative was to continue treatment and potentially see things improve or if things went badly see Dorothy's health decline even faster.

God once again reinforced to me and the children during this time that if He said 'Otherwise', that is, He decided to take Dorothy to be with Himself, He would be right there with us and He would give us the strength we needed to go through it all at that moment in time.

For the children and I to see Dorothy in such pain, especially with the reaction to the last treatment, was very hard on us, not to mention what Dorothy personally had to endure on a daily basis. Everything that was being done was in the hope that the treatment would extend Dorothy's life for longer but was it to continue to be at the expense of her quality of life? Dorothy had reached a point where she needed significant amounts of rest every day. She could no longer walk for too long, such was the swelling of her legs, ankles and feet, yet she soldiered on still wanting to look after our family.

As a family we were going through a very difficult time, however the support we were getting was fantastic. Many people provided meals via a meal roster which was organised at work. My Year 12 Home Group students gave a gift to Dorothy and me that was a beautiful and thoughtful gesture and left me speechless! It was a gift voucher for the shops and to see a movie. For my family it was also very meaningful. Dorothy was so touched emotionally when she read the card she couldn't stop shaking. In all of this we continued to trust in God and chose to allow Him to let things unfold according to His plans and purposes. God was the one in control and again His thoughts and ways are higher than our thoughts and ways. Significant verses that we held onto during this time are listed below.

Psalm 90:12 *So teach us to number our days, That we may gain a heart of wisdom. (NKJV)*

Psalm 31:15 *My times are in Your hands; Deliver me from the hand of my enemies, And from those who persecute me. (NKJV)*

Philippians 1:19 *For I know that as you pray for me and the Spirit of Jesus Christ helps me this will lead to my deliverance. (NLT)*

All of our lives are truly in His hands and we knew that as people prayed for us and the Holy Spirit helped us we would continue to experience God's deliverance through this time whatever that might look like. God would continue to look after my family and in all of this Dorothy was safe in the palm of His hand. This was something that Dorothy held onto throughout her suffering.

Chapter 15: Count It All Joy

As Dorothy's health continued to deteriorate, during the final month of her life, it was a passage from James that really helped strengthen our mindset as a family.

James 1:2-6 *"My brethren count it all joy when you fall into various trials, knowing that the testing of your faith produces patience. But let patience have its perfect work, that you may be perfect and complete, lacking nothing. If any of you lacks wisdom, let him ask of God, who gives to all liberally and without reproach, and it will be given to him. But let him ask in faith, with no doubting, for he who doubts is like a wave of the sea driven and tossed by the wind."* *(NKJV)*

When I first read this passage I found it very challenging, especially when considering the trial of life we were going through. It seemed very hard to consider it all joy when you see someone you love in such pain. After further study of this passage my understanding of what it meant changed somewhat.

What we were going through was the testing of our faith. Our trial and suffering was testing our fidelity (loyalty, faithfulness), integrity, virtue and constancy, towards God. This was the cause or occasion for joy because we knew that through it all our faith was being made perfect.

What we were going through was producing patience, that is, a cheerful and hopeful endurance and steadfastness that we would not be swerved from God's purposes in and through our lives. God was making us, through our trials, complete and faithful servants to Him who would not be swerved from His plans and purposes. It was this that we were to count, deem, consider all joy. This was the cause or occasion for joy that the trial, adversity and suffering we were going through was bringing about, the completion and finish of God's perfect work in our lives.

Knowing that what we were going through was bringing about a work of God in our lives that was developing faith and character, was something to be cheerful about and consider with calm delight. What we were going through was producing patience in our lives such that we might live with cheerful endurance no matter what came our way. This trial was producing in us a characteristic that we would not be swerved from God's plans and purposes and our loyalty to Him in terms of both faith and piety (holiness) could not be shifted. No matter what the outcome, we would serve the Lord. This was something to be excited about. What we were going through was doing something in our heart, mind and lives that would never have happened if we weren't going through what we were at that time.

It wasn't the suffering or the cancer itself that we were to consider or count all joy, but rather it was what God was doing through the midst of it all that we were to consider all joy. God did amazing things in our relationship with Him, our relationship with one another and our relationship with our children and through it all He has used and is still using our lives to inspire and motivate others!

My family has always been in God's hands. No lines were drawn, no deals were made. We gave our lives to God regardless of the outcome and we know from experience even in the midst of suffering that God is good. God owes us nothing but we continue to owe Him everything. This is the resolve that was and still is in our hearts, and no matter what, we choose to serve the Lord. We are so grateful and thankful for the time with Dorothy that God gave us in this life, and one thing we know is that ultimately our future with her in Christ will be of a far longer duration than the past we have spent with her - all eternity!

Chapter 16: A Blessing For Dorothy In Her Final Month

Below I have outlined a summary of an amazing divine appointment which God orchestrated through my golf club championships. This was a blessing to Dorothy that she and I never saw coming in the middle of one of life's greatest trials for us.

The first round of the club championships happened on Saturday the 1st of February 2014. I went out and had a terrible round and shot a 91. I was in 'A Grade' which included handicaps between 8 and 13. I was 12 shots off the pace after the first round. I then went out the following week and had another bad round and shot 89. Fortunately for me the day reached a temperature over 40°C and play was abandoned which meant none of the scores that day counted.

On the 15th of February the second round was replayed and I shot an 82. I went from being 12 shots off the pace to 4 shots. On the 22nd of February I was due to play at 7.00 am in the morning but got a wakeup call from God at around 4.25 am. I got up and went to my office and started to pray. While praying I received a very strong flow of words deep within that said, "Play to win." I couldn't shake it and I knew that for the final two rounds I was to go out and play with this mindset. As I was thinking about this flow of words I started to think about what I would say if I did win and so I started to write my speech! The speech I wrote is written below.

Many of us play for different reasons; some to have the lowest possible handicap, some for fitness and others for the social aspects. My reasons changed at the start of 2012. My wife was diagnosed with a brain tumour as a result of secondary breast cancer, and at that time it was like I started living day to day with a foggy mind. I felt like I had a permanent weight across my shoulders. Only two things would bring about relief from that cloudiness and weight and that was playing golf and running. I would play golf and forget about the circumstances of life and enjoy the company of those I would play alongside. For a brief time every week I would find relief through physical activity and meeting people on the golf course.

I want to thank all of you for being a part of that relief because many of you are people I have met and played with along the way. My wife is still battling on and things are getting very serious so this weekend I played to win so that I could get my name on that board and every time I see my name there I will remember how much she means to me and also how much all of my friends here at this golf course mean to me. I also hope that when you see my name on that board you will think of my wife who has an amazing faith and trust in God in the midst of pain and suffering. She is a fantastic woman and I played to win so that you might also know about her story.

I also know that I can continue to come to this golf club and know that I have friends who will support me. We still have hope in the midst of suffering and when any of you face tough circumstances I hope you see my name and think of my wife and ask God for help. I no longer have the cloudy head all the time or the weight and pressure of life across my shoulders but I still have my friends. Thank you for this opportunity and I pray that I might continue to find enjoyment on the golf course by playing alongside many of you. (Completed by about 5.30 am)

I then proceeded to go out and play at 7.00 am that morning and I shot another 82. I knew this was a good score and the club championship works in such a way that after three rounds the top 8 out of approximately 100 competitors make it to the final round. I got a call at 6.00 pm that day to let me know that I had qualified and I was playing around 12.20 pm the next day. They also told me I was 2 shots in the lead!

I went out the following day with the words, "Play to Win" still reverberating in my mind. At the start of the round there were two guys in my group 2 shots behind me and one other guy 6 shots behind me. After 9 holes I was level in score with one other player and the other two guys were 3 and 6 shots behind us respectively. The game was close and up there for three of us to win.

On the 12th hole I played a Par 3 and hit an iron 2 metres from the pin and then putted the ball which agonizingly stopped on the lip of the hole. I waited and proceeded to walk around the hole at which point when I turned my head away just for a second it dropped in!

On the 15th hole I knew things were really going my way. I was playing a Par 4 and I had hit a nice tee off and had a second shot at the green over water. Unfortunately my ball was in a divot filled with sand so the lie wasn't that great. When I hit the ball it looked like it wasn't going to make it over the water. It landed on the mud bank on the other side of the water and most times the ball would hit and roll back into the water and that would cost me a couple of shots. My ball amazingly must have hit the only stone in the mud bank and bounced forward away from the water another 20m. I then chipped the ball fairly close to the hole, made the putt and finished with par! Had the ball gone in the water it could have cost me 2 or 3 shots.

I finished off the round after that, playing fairly solid golf and when I finished I didn't know really where I stood overall. It didn't take too long though to find out I had won the 'A grade' club championship by six shots! I put the golf clubs away, grabbed my speech written in the early hours of Saturday morning and had a quick read. I gave the speech, not exactly the same as I had written because it was off the cuff and I couldn't remember it exactly but I still honoured Dorothy and friends at the golf club. The speech was received really well and the guy after me said how inspirational it was and he proceeded to thank his family, friends and dedicated his win to someone.

After the speeches were done I had a lot of people come up and thank me and tell me how much they appreciated what I said. One guy shook my hand three times - he just didn't know what to say plus he had probably had a little too much to drink! Another guy told me how he was only given three months to live and five years on he was still going thanks to the support of friends. This was a divine opportunity that God had mapped out for me and through it He was able to touch the lives of others.

When I got home I told Dorothy and the children and they were very happy. Dorothy outwardly burst into tears and she said that she had never felt so loved, appreciated and honoured as she did right then. How amazing is God? Is He in control? I know He is! I still thank God for this amazing sequence of events and letting things unfold the way they did. This was definitely an example of how in the midst of suffering God was still able to move and bless us and others.

Chapter 17: The Final Week - A Defining Moment

The focus of the final week of Dorothy's life written here is not so much the ugliness of what happened but rather the beauty we saw through the ugliness. A passage that Jayden selected to read at the celebration service for Dorothy from Ecclesiastes is written below and helped us to put everything in perspective.

Ecclesiastes 3:1-4 *To everything there is a season, A time for every purpose under heaven: A time to be born, And a time to die; A time to plant, And a time to pluck what is planted; A time to kill, And a time to heal; A time to break down, And a time to build up; A time to weep, And a time to laugh; A time to mourn, And a time to dance; (NKJV)*

One of the things that I wanted the children to concentrate on in the last month of Dorothy's life was for each one of them to tell mum how much they loved her every day. Why? We didn't know how much longer she was going to be with us and I wanted the kids' final memories of Dorothy to be based around them telling her how much they loved her. I never wanted them to look back and think that they should have said more to her during this time. At times they wrote letters and read them to her, making sure they expressed why she was so special to them. It was also important for Dorothy to hear their genuine expressions of love for her.

For those people who knew Dorothy well it was a shock how quickly she went. We knew her health was deteriorating but her final week in this life saw the illness advance with a speed we never expected. God had revealed to me in prayer it was going to happen quicker than I would think and I never understood what that meant until the final week.

On Thursday the 20th of March 2014 one week before she died I can still remember Dorothy standing at the door step and waving goodbye to the boys and myself as we drove off to school with

Todd, a colleague and close friend that I car pool with. The following day on the Friday, it was Nicole's birthday, a close friend to Dorothy. Dorothy wanted to go out with Nicole and Jill (another close friend) and I didn't think she could manage it but she was determined. One thing about Dorothy was that when she had her mind set on something it was difficult to shake her. It was only a short amount of time that she went out for and she was exhausted when she got back but she did it! Now it is a memory that Nicole and Jill will cherish.

On Saturday, Dorothy was slowing down a lot but she was still able to shower herself. She was sleeping a lot at this point, most of the day in fact but we were able to talk and chat for short periods of time. The nights were considerably more difficult because the pain was greater then. I was looking after Dorothy by myself at this point with the children at home as well. I was giving her oral medication whenever she needed it but it started to become apparent the medication was not enough. I was constantly in touch with Eastern Palliative Care and they had to come out to administer morphine intravenously in order to deal with Dorothy's pain.

Dorothy was very tired most of the day on Sunday, and again continued to sleep a considerable amount of time. I remember sitting in bed with her and asking her how she was going. Where was she at? Her response was, "I am safe in His hands." Dorothy continued to hold onto her belief that God had her in the palm of

His hand even in this final week. I then asked her what she was thinking about when she was still and just lying there and she said, "Oh nothing, nothing at all."

By Monday Dorothy needed help getting to the bathroom and could only hold a conversation for a couple of minutes. She was able to communicate, just not for that long. By this time the pain was intense and Dorothy had been crying and groaning throughout the previous night. I was beside myself because I didn't know what to do. Eastern Palliative Care were still supporting us but the time between calls and when they arrived meant Dorothy was suffering for too long. Oral medication was useless and I couldn't administer medication intravenously. In my desperation I reached a point of recognising I couldn't keep Dorothy at home with the situation the way it was.

I rang Sue, Dorothy's sister, who is a nurse, and told her what was happening. She left from Casterton very soon after and travelled five hours to get to Melbourne. After she arrived she said that she would administer the medication to Dorothy by injection. I gave her the choice given Dorothy was her sister. Dorothy had always wanted to spend her final days at home and I had wanted to honour that, but when it got to the point of seeing her suffer so much it was only because Sue was willing to administer morphine that Dorothy remained at home. I am so thankful that Sue was willing to do this. Karen, also one of Dorothy's sisters was a huge support during this time, helping to keep our family going in what was a very difficult time.

Dorothy by the end of the day on Tuesday could no longer have a normal conversation. She was able to answer questions and she spoke so gently and beautifully. For example, I asked her if she had a good day and she responded, "Yeeeeah." I then asked her if she got much done and her response was, "Noooo." These are beautiful memories for me and even now as I think about the way she spoke at this time I am brought to tears.

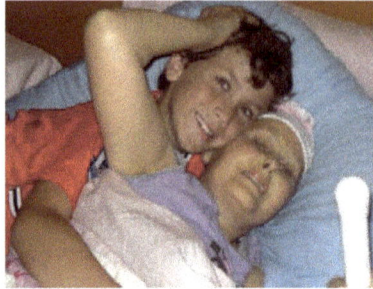

By Wednesday Dorothy could only utter sounds particularly when it was in recognition of someone. She wasn't moving from the bed at all by this time. I remember sitting beside the bed on a number of different occasions, hoping for a glimpse of recognition. I cherished those moments where she recognised me. It was during this time I had the smallest of glimpses of what it meant for someone to have to go through watching a loved one with Alzheimer's disease. To be beside someone you love and have them no longer recognise you is very painful. I only had a small glimpse but for someone having to go through that for months, even years, must be so hard.

On Thursday the 27th March 2014, the final day that Dorothy was to have in this life, although we didn't know it at the time, the boys went off to school with Todd and before they went they gave a hug and a kiss goodbye to Dorothy and there was recognition and she hugged each of them. I went a little later in the morning to finalise some things at work and leave work for the next day. Dorothy in that moment reached up and hugged me goodbye. It was very special.

By the time I got home it was apparent that Dorothy was labouring in her breathing. Her mum and dad were travelling to Melbourne from Merino with my brother in law and his wife and I was just praying they would make it in time. At this point we were having a steady stream of visitors who were coming to see Dorothy and say goodbye. I had let people know by email that Dorothy's health was deteriorating very quickly. This was evident by the fact that people were still trying to text her as normal, expecting her to respond to them. We gave people time to sit and just express to Dorothy how much they loved her. Dorothy's parents arrived during daylight hours and we took them straight in. Dorothy got to see them! By this time many of Dorothy's family had arrived in Melbourne and were staying nearby. It was a precious thing for Dorothy's friends and family to come and sit beside her and say goodbye.

It came time to put the children to bed. Kelby went in first and gave Mummy a big hug and kiss and he went off to sleep. Jayden went next and he gave Mum a long hug and a big kiss and went to bed. Kalani was the final one to come in and say goodnight and she came in and gave Dorothy a kiss on the cheek and said, "Goodnight Mum, love you" and turned to go to bed. At this point Dorothy called out and raised her arm. I called Kalani back and Dorothy raised her arm again and hugged her. I told Kalani how special that moment was and she said, "That's because I'm special!" The fact is she is special and Dorothy wanted her to know that and Kalani will remember that moment for the rest of her life. This was the last major movement Dorothy made before she died.

At around 10:30 pm I had just finished a Bible study and was reading while sitting next to Dorothy and her breathing was still laboured. As I was sitting beside her I had a burning within my stomach region and a real prophetic unction rose up within me. For those who don't know what a prophetic word is, it is when God quickens something in someone where He gives them the words that He wants them to say on His behalf. I received a word from God for Dorothy at this time and I have written this word below as I remember it. It is important to understand that it was like the words were flowing from deep within and coming from the stomach region to my mouth. My mind was aware of what I was saying but I was not controlling the words that I was speaking forth, although I was fully aware of them.

"Dorothy you have impacted the lives of many people in life and the life you have lived will continue to impact the lives of many people even in death. The ripples from your life will continue onwards and outwards like throwing a rock in water, and will continue to vibrate throughout eternity. Know this that through your suffering lives have been touched according to My plans and My purposes. I have done a work in Alistair's life because of what you have had to endure. The ripples from your life have touched him and changed his life forever and the affects still flow on. In his work place students' lives, people he works alongside and parents have all been impacted because of the ripples from your life and they will continue on. You have imparted a Godly heritage into your children and again the effects will flow on both now and in years to come. The life you have lived and the example you have set have given them soft hearts towards others. You have been an example and a testimony to your family of what it means to live for God, even in the midst of pain and suffering and your life has drawn them closer to Me than ever before. The ripples of your life go out and will continue to go out through Alistair, the kids and your family. The strength of your faith and your resolve to live for Me has given hope to so many of your friends and people outside of your family that you have come to know. The ripples from your life have touched the lives of others and in turn because of your ripples, ripples are going out from their lives and once again these ripples will continue to vibrate throughout all eternity. Well done good and faithful servant. Enter into the joy of the Lord."

It was at this exact moment as I voiced these words on God's behalf that Dorothy gave two breaths (gargles) and then breathed her last with one long sigh! I now knew beyond a shadow of a doubt that these words were from God and the reality of God came to a whole new level in my life as a result of this experience. To know that God was so intimately involved with Dorothy leaving this life and passing into eternity is one of the greatest defining moments in my life!

This is a memory that I will hold for the rest of my life. The final thing that Dorothy heard in this life was God speaking to her about the value, significance and impact of her life. Through suffering look at what God has been able to accomplish. Look at the ripples!

Kalani explained at the celebration service for Dorothy why we chose to call it a celebration service. As she explained, we chose to call it this because Mum has entered into the joy of the Lord. She is in heaven rejoicing with God, angels and believers who have gone before her. She is celebrating and we have a hope in Christ that we will see her again! She is no longer suffering anymore pain.

1 Thessalonians 4:13-18 *And now, dear brothers and sisters, we want you to know what will happen to the believers who have fallen asleep so you will not grieve like people who have no hope, as if the grave were the last word. For since we believe that Jesus died and was raised to life again, we also believe that when Jesus returns, God will most certainly bring back with Him the believers who have died in Jesus. For this we say to you by the word of the Lord, that we who are alive and remain until the coming of the Lord will by no means precede those who are asleep. For the Lord Himself will descend from heaven with a shout, with the voice of an archangel, and with the trumpet of God. And the dead in Christ will rise first. Then we who are alive and remain shall be caught up together with them in the clouds to meet the Lord in the air. And thus we shall always be with the Lord. Therefore <u>comfort</u> one another with these words. (This passage is a blending of the New King James Version, the New Living Translation and the Message Bibles. We call it the PTV - The Pitman Translated Version!)*

As mentioned previously, the word that we held onto for over a year and a half was, "Dorothy is not going anywhere unless God says 'Otherwise.'" What we didn't know was what 'Otherwise' meant. Putting it all together God was saying, "Dorothy is not going anywhere unless I say, 'Well done good and faithful servant enter into the joy of the Lord.'"

Chapter 18: The Moments After Dorothy's Passing

Moments after Dorothy breathed her last, Dorothy's sisters, Sue and Karen came into the room and I said, "I think she's gone." Sue checked for a pulse and confirmed that Dorothy had passed from this life into eternity. I put my head down near to hers and howled. It was guttural. There was sorrow as I realized my wife had died yet I had an unshakeable knowledge that she had entered into the joy of the Lord. My wife and best friend whom I had known for just over twenty-five years and married to for almost twenty-one years had left this life to be with God in the most amazing way possible.

Dorothy when she breathed her last had left this life in a sleeping position on her side and looked exactly like she was asleep. I went and woke up Kalani and said to her, "Mum has gone to sleep and she has woken up in eternity." As Kalani took this in there were tears and sadness and she came in to the bedroom and looked at Mum and then went to stand with Sue and Karen.

I then went and got Jayden and told him that Mummy had gone to sleep and that she had woken up in eternity. He cried and came in and looked at Dorothy and went over and kissed her goodbye and then went and stood with Kalani.

I then went and got Kelby and once again I said, "Mummy has fallen asleep and woken up in eternity." He turned to me and said, "Mummy has gone to heaven?" I replied, "That's right." Again tears and sadness, and I took him in to the bedroom and said he could go over to Mummy. Kelby went over and gave her big cuddle and a big kiss.

Kelby read a passage at the celebration service from Psalm 150. The reason he chose this passage was because he wanted to praise God for Mummy's life and because she was now in heaven praising God.

Psalm 150:1-6 *Praise the LORD! Praise God in His sanctuary; praise Him in His mighty heaven! Praise Him for His mighty works; praise His unequaled greatness! Praise Him with a blast of the ram's horn; praise Him with the lyre and harp! Praise Him with the tambourine and dancing; Praise Him with strings and flutes! Praise Him with a clash of cymbals; praise Him with loud clanging cymbals. Let everything that breathes sing praises to the LORD! Praise the LORD! (NLT)*

I then took him over to everyone else and we stood and hugged one another with a big family hug and cried. It was sad but there was joy. Side by side we saw sadness with joy, beauty with ugliness, pain and suffering with release and freedom.

After this the children and I left the room and Karen and Sue dressed Dorothy in clothes that we chose for her to be buried in. Jayden helped pick the cardigan and top, Kalani chose the skirt, Kelby chose the shoes and I chose the rings and jewelry for her to have. Karen and Sue dressed her beautifully. When we came back to the room she was lying on the bed with her arms across her chest holding a lovely pink flower. She looked beautiful and she had a slight smile on her lips and she lay there so peacefully. We all stood around the bed and just looked at her and cried. It truly was a 'Snow White/ Sleeping Beauty' scenario.

Our families all came over in the early hours of the morning to just look at her one last time and appreciate how beautiful she was. She was truly beautiful in life and also in death and again another memory I will hold for the rest of my life.

Chapter 19: Some Reflections On Dorothy's Life

Dorothy was a person who sometimes looked at her life and said, "I'm just a mum, I'm just a housewife." God saw her as so much more as did I and the children - way more - and that was the final thing she heard. Her life fulfilled the plans and purposes of God. She ran her race. The ripples from her life will continue vibrating throughout eternity.

We found that throughout our journey of suffering there were many different views and voices as to what we should be doing and how we should be seeking God through it all. However, the one thing that we can say is that we did what God placed on our hearts to do. We were obedient to Him and Dorothy and I had discussed this in depth and we had no regrets. We were thankful and grateful for all that God had done in us and through us.

A close friend from work sent me a verse in November 2013 and the verse was **Isaiah 43:2**.

Isaiah 43:2 *When you pass through the waters I will be with you; And through the rivers, they shall not overflow you. When you walk through the fire you shall not be burned, Nor shall the flame scorch you. (NKJV)*

She said God told her to give this verse to me and He would show me what it means. I had no idea at first so I asked God to show me. He brought back to me a picture that Dorothy had been given by a close friend where Dorothy was passing between walls of waters from one side to the other. She walked across on dry land with the water held back and the enemy couldn't touch her. She had her long brown curly hair and beautiful clothing and she was turning back and waving as she walked across. This picture was to me Dorothy passing through from this life to the next and God was with her, protecting her.

The second part of the verse related to the children and I. We were going through turbulent rivers but they would not overflow us. We were walking through the flames but they would not burn us or scorch us. Even though God had called Dorothy to Himself God was going to look after us through the turbulent waters and fires. He would not let us drown or be burnt.

This was the picture that I put with the above verse in November 2013 and God brought it back to my memory during the last week of Dorothy's life. At the time in November I had no idea when this verse was going to be fulfilled and I chose to just sit on it. God had also added at this time to a word we had received great strength from a month earlier and it was, *"I am with you My son, I am with Dorothy, I am with your children and I am with your family. If I say 'Otherwise', that is I call Dorothy unto Myself, I will give you strength in that moment in time to walk through it. **I am with you!**"*

Dorothy has now passed through the water that separates life from eternity. God is with me and my family and we shall not be burnt. God is truly good. He owes me nothing but I owe Him everything!

We now have a confidence in God that He will continue to help the children and I get through each and every day. We have a hope that we will see Dorothy again in heaven and the reality is I will continue to see Dorothy in the children. In Kelby I see her mischievous and joyful nature. In Jayden I see her sensitivity, love and care for others. In Kalani I see her beauty, her love of baking, her gentleness and her love of hoarding, but I won't go there!

Dorothy was buried in Merino on the 8th of April and I remember going back to the cemetery on the 10th of April (it would have been our twenty-first anniversary) and standing by the grave. I knew that spiritually Dorothy was no longer there (she is in heaven) but her earthly body was still there. In that moment the resolve in my heart to serve God and commit my life to Him afresh was the strongest it had ever been and all I wanted in life was to get what Dorothy got, those amazing words, "Well done good and faithful servant. Enter into the joy of the Lord." To have lived your life, accomplishing God's plans and purposes is what truly counts with me.

The suffering that Dorothy endured has set ripples in motion that have led to me seeking God like never before. It is my prayer that the ripples from her life might also continue on through you. May your lives impact the lives of others as the ripples of her life continue on through you.

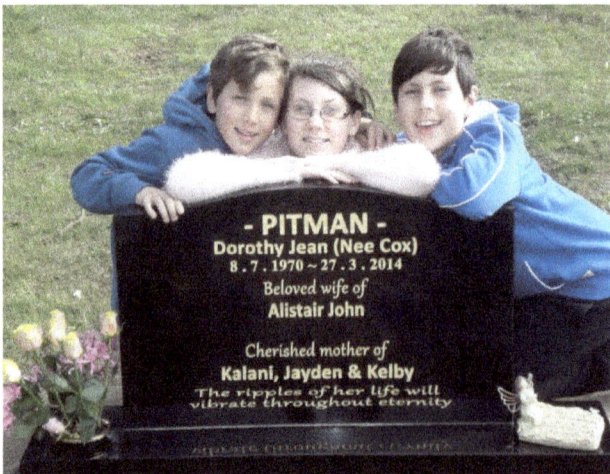

Chapter 20: Life Goes On No Matter How Hard Things Are

In the first few weeks after Dorothy left this life people were genuinely concerned about me and the children and the support was overwhelming. Meals came flooding in as we had to deal with all of the things that have to be done when a loved one leaves this life. The celebration service had to be organised, burial arrangements finalised and letting all of the different groups and organisations know that Dorothy had died was just the beginning.

The main question that was asked of us during this time was, "How are you going and how are the children going?" I have tried to capture what things were like for us during this time immediately after Dorothy's death and hopefully give you a snap shot of how God was with us during this time just like He promised He would be.

We were doing reasonably well given the circumstances. I had lost my wife and best friend and the children had lost their mother and the linchpin of our family. Yet in the midst of this we had an assurance that God was with us. We continued to hold onto the word that God gave us in November 2013, which I outlined in the previous chapter, where He said to us, *"I am with you My son, I am with Dorothy, I am with your children and I am with your family. If I say 'Otherwise', that is I call Dorothy unto Myself, I will give you strength in that moment in time to walk through it. **I am with you!**"*

Even in the midst of pain, suffering and grief we knew God was with us. We experienced His presence in a tangible way and we opened ourselves up to the support of our community and friends whether it was family, friends, church, workplace or school.

Life as we knew it had changed dramatically but we established new routines in the home so that we could get things done that needed to be done by helping one another. Practical things that we had taken for granted before, like meals, washing up, cleaning up, keeping the house in order, washing clothes and the like were all practical things that we slowly got on top of. If something needed to be done we put one person in charge and everyone else helped that person to do it.

I looked after meals and my plan was to slowly wean ourselves off meals being provided by others and cook more and more meals each week. Jayden became responsible for dishes and clean up but everyone got in and helped by washing their own dishes and putting them on the rack or in the dishwasher. Jayden put them away. Kalani became responsible for the washing of clothes but we all got in and helped hang them out to dry and bring them in. Kalani then sorted the clothes into piles and we all had to put our own clothes away. Kelby became responsible for the dog, setting the table, helping everyone else and even kindly offered to look after the iPad and X-Box, which I declined! I assured him I would find some more responsibilities for him. My mum helped out in an amazing way by cleaning the house. She has blessed us by demonstrating her love for us in a very real and practical way.

Each new day provided fresh challenges but it was also part of a new beginning for us. We had only just tasted and had a small glimpse of what God had in store for us as a family. We were safe in His hands and under His protection. We continued to walk through the fire, knowing the flame would not touch or scorch us. We were going through the turbulent waters knowing that they would not overflow us.

Around our meal times each of us shared what God had spoken to us from our own personal reading each day. It was a pleasure and a joy to hear the children's level of faith and trust in God even in the midst of that which we were going through.

Chapter 21: Triggers, The Rollercoaster And A Picture

At first we experienced 'triggers' every day, that is memories that reminded us of Dorothy and one of the best ways to describe our lives was a little like a rollercoaster. We experienced highs as we remembered special things about Dorothy but we also experienced lows as we approached certain things knowing Dorothy was no longer going to be there. Easter and Mother's day were classic examples and all we could do was acknowledge the wonderful times we had shared in the past, cherish those memories, reflect on them and then let them go. The highs and lows of a roller coaster are frequent at the beginning of the ride but as the ride goes on the oscillation around that central point decreases.

Our highs and lows were many and frequent at the start and I was brought to tears by triggers most of the early days after Dorothy's passing, but I learnt to welcome those triggers because they were memories of a wonderful woman. The key was not to let those triggers be like a whirlpool that sucked me or the children down into a pit of despair, but rather to accept them for what they were, living memories of Dorothy in our heart.

A picture that I received while praying which really helped the children and me was that of a baseballer who had the role of catching the pitches made by the thrower. The catcher has a big mitt and when he catches the ball the mitt absorbs most of the impact and there might be some discomfort depending on the speed and intensity of the pitch, but once the pitch has been caught and the impact of it is absorbed the ball is let go.

The ball pitched is like a trigger coming to us that brings either some past memory or a reminder of some event that we have shared together in the past such as our wedding anniversary, birthdays or Mother's day. The mitt is God helping us absorb the impact of those triggers and we accept those triggers, acknowledge them and reflect on them, but we then also let them go. We accept them for what they are, and that is memories related to a very special and wonderful woman.

A verse that I was reminded of at this time was **2 Chronicles 16:9.**

2 Chronicles 16:9 *For the eyes of the Lord run to and fro throughout the whole earth, to show Himself strong on behalf of those whose heart is loyal to Him ... (NKJV)*

The children and I took this to heart and all we wanted to do was make sure that our hearts stayed loyal to Him in all that we were going through and we knew that He would show Himself strong on our behalf as a result. This has been our experience.

Something I received in prayer during this time were the words, "Dorothy is with Me and she is just so pleased, so excited and so joyful knowing that the pain and suffering she endured set the wheels in motion for you to start seeking Me like never before and has led to the change that has come about in your life, the children's lives and in the lives of so many others." I knew Dorothy had entered into the joy of the Lord and to know a small taste of what brings her joy once more revealed to me how truly wonderful she was in this life and still is in heaven!

Chapter 22: Intimacy Lost

The thing that I found the hardest in those first few weeks after Dorothy's transition from this life to the next was that I was no longer able to share with Dorothy those day to day happenings, as well as that which God had placed on my heart and mind each day, nor was I receiving an understanding of where she was at or a knowledge of what was going on in her life. I was missing sharing life with someone that I had come to know so intimately.

This whole area of intimacy with Dorothy was lost and I don't mean physical intimacy. I mean the kind that comes from sharing your heart with another. For me, I experience great joy from finding out and knowing that which is in God's heart and mind and then having the opportunity to share that with another. It was like my joy was made complete when I got to share with Dorothy all that God was revealing through His word and she was always so excited both to listen and to share her heart as well.

The best definition I have heard for intimacy is, *'Intimacy involves knowing one's heart without limitation and sharing one's heart without reservation.'* (*Your Destiny* - Ivan and Isabella Allum - *page 141*)

Dorothy and I had applied this to our relationship in a far greater measure than ever before, especially after the cancer went secondary in February 2012. This is why I am able to say that Dorothy and I became closer as a couple, closer than we had ever been before, during this time.

 It was significant that a friend said to me that Dorothy and I were in agreement and on the same page throughout this period of suffering, except in relation to the last round of chemotherapy that she took. The Oncologist wanted to have one more shot at treatment and so did Dorothy, because that effectively would be the last chance Dorothy would have at fighting the cancer. I on the other hand had seen up close and personal how ugly the second last treatment had been on her and I did not want her to have to go through the same level of pain again and nor did I want the children to see it. I thought another round would potentially leave her in a position she wouldn't recover from. I realised for myself I just wanted to see her live for as long as possible without the pain of treatment. Apart from this our level of intimacy was wonderful and to have now lost this was truly a hard thing for me.

I have learnt how vital it is to have close friends surrounding me to face the grief and to be able to talk through what is going on. I know that if God had not led me to developing close friendships over the last eighteen months of Dorothy's life I would have struggled far more than I did because I would have been doing it alone.

In hindsight I believe things unfolded in such a way that left Dorothy leaving this life with greater speed and possibly lessened the pain and suffering she might have had to endure otherwise. The last treatment was clearly what pushed the liver too far and she basically died from the liver shutting down completely. One of Dorothy's prayers was that if God was to say 'Otherwise', in other words it was time for her to leave this life and enter into eternity to be with Him, she didn't want it to be a drawn out time in hospital and God answered this in a powerful way.

Even though we disagreed on what should happen, I supported her and the Oncologist in what she wanted to do because her desire was clearly to continue living for longer than a few months even if it was only a small possibility. Reading her journal over the final month of her life revealed to me how strong her desire to live was and how much she wanted to continue to be with me and the children even though she couldn't do a lot anymore. Her heart before God was so honest and simple.

One of Dorothy's greatest concerns was how I would go raising three children alone and how would they cope without her. She had expressed this to me a number of months before she died and I know in the end that she knew because of God's word to us that He would be right there giving the strength to the children and myself in that moment of time, if and when He said 'Otherwise'.

He has been with the children and with me in a real and tangible way. It hasn't been easy but He has given us strength. To know where Dorothy is now without a shadow of a doubt has been an amazing source of comfort for the children and me.

Chapter 23: This Life Is Not About What I Want

One of the major shifts that happened in my thinking in those first few weeks after Dorothy died was that this life was not about what I wanted. It was not about fulfilling my desires, my wants, my needs, etc. but rather it was all about doing according to what was in God's heart and mind. A verse that has always had special meaning to me is found in **1 Samuel 2:35**.

1 Samuel 2:35 *Then I will raise up for Myself a faithful priest who shall do according to what is in My heart and mind. I will build him a sure house, and he shall walk before My anointed forever. (NKJV)*

The resolve in my heart was that this life was not about what I wanted, rather it was all about doing according to what was in His heart and mind. I desired to be a righteous man, a person who walked in close fellowship with God.

Genesis 6:9 *This is the account of Noah and his family. Noah was a righteous man, the only blameless person living on earth at the time and he walked in close fellowship with God. (NLT)*

As I have studied what it means to be a righteous man, the definition that came to me as a result of this study was two-fold. Firstly, a person is made righteous before God when they accept Christ, that is, they are brought into a position of right standing before God because they have accepted what Jesus did for them. Secondly, a righteous man is one whose way of thinking, feeling and acting becomes wholly conformed to the will of God day to day. The key to being able to do this is what we see with Noah and that is walking in close fellowship with God.

I know from my own experience over the last year or so that as I have been spending more and more time with God that is the only place I want to be. Every time I am woken up in the early hours of the morning it is another opportunity to meet with Him and find out

His heart and mind. Once again the verse from Psalm 22:8 (NLT) springs to mind and the words I hear, according to the Pitman Translated Version, are "Alistair, come and talk with Me." and the attitude and response of my heart is, "Lord I am coming, Lord I am there!" There is no place I would rather be.

My life, my body, all that I am is to be a living sacrifice to God to be used by Him so that He can accomplish infinitely, abundantly, over and above, and so much more than I ever thought possible through me. My life is in God's hands available for His service and use. I truly do desire to be a vessel that He can flow through and so strike chords that will continue to vibrate throughout eternity.

Chapter 24: A Divine Encounter

One of the hardest points in the grieving process came for me around the two month mark after Dorothy's passing. I had been missing being able to share with Dorothy all that doing life together with someone else involves, including sharing day to day happenings. Along with this I had also been missing the depth of Dorothy's love for me. Dorothy's love for me accepted me regardless of my faults and weaknesses. Having known Dorothy for twenty-five years and being married for almost twenty-one, I had not realised how much I had taken her love for granted. It was always present and always there and I didn't intentionally take it for granted. I just didn't realise how great her love for me was until it wasn't there anymore.

I have come to realise the fact that it cannot be replaced. No one else will ever be able to replace that love, because that was Dorothy's gift to me. Her love for me was unique. It was special and I was really wrestling with this reality at the time. Even though I had close friends, they couldn't replace what I was missing and it would have been wrong of me to expect them to, as well as impossible. The depth of sorrow and anguish that I was experiencing at this time was immense.

It was from this place that God really ministered to me. I went out for a run and I was mulling over this whole idea of how much I was missing the depth of Dorothy's love for me. It felt like the quickest 10 kilometres I had ever run because I was so lost in my thoughts. At the end of my run I arrived at my driveway and I was thinking about grief and all of its various stages in relation to Dorothy when all of a sudden I experienced God's manifest presence in a powerful way. It was like a blanket wrapped around me and I felt the firmness and warm pressure of that blanket. At the same time I received the words "Let it go, let it go, let it go." By the time I reached the end of the driveway and got to the garage door the 'blanket' lifted and it was like the weight of missing Dorothy's love for me dropped away. I just let go. The absence of Dorothy's love for me was filled by the Holy Spirit and I was released from a troubled mind. I still missed Dorothy but the depth of that anguish and sorrow had left. This encounter really brought a whole new meaning to **John 14:26-27**.

John 14:26-27 *But the Helper* (Comforter)*, the Holy Spirit, whom the Father will send in My name, He will teach you all things, and bring to your remembrance all things that I said to you. Peace I leave with you, My peace I give to you; not as the world gives do I give to you. Let not your heart be troubled, neither let it be afraid. (NKJV)*

The Holy Spirit is truly my Comforter and He has continued to help me in so many ways since then. One thing that I was warned about was that 6-7 weeks after Dorothy had gone would be when reality really would start to set in, and I can say I found this to be true. Life goes on for everyone, as it does and should, and naturally the support of family and friends lessens. Although the reality of Dorothy being gone was heightened, one thing I know was that God was still with me and the children. Prior to Dorothy's passing one of my biggest concerns, like Dorothy, was how was I going to cope raising three children alone as a single dad? He has shown me in a powerful way that I am whole and complete as a single dad and more than capable of raising three children because He is right there with me even if my cooking is somewhat lacking!

Kalani, Jayden and Kelby continued to do amazingly well through all of the events during this time and the fact that we were open and honest as a family around the meal table to talk about how each of us was going really helped all of us support each other. They appreciated being able to move on during this time without having to explain so often how they were coping. The devotions we had after tea were gold and each of them working through their own devotional books loved sharing what they had received from God each day. Their faith has become stronger through this whole experience and to see Kalani and Jayden enter into praise and worship during a church service in a far deeper way is fantastic. Was God able to help all of us through this time? Absolutely!

The final words Dorothy wrote in her journal, exactly one week before she entered into eternity were, *'Bless my family Lord, Alistair, boys and Kalani.'* He has and He will continue to do so!

Chapter 25: Understanding The Grieving Process

My understanding of the grieving process steadily grew as I examined both what the Bible had to say, as well as other written material on the subject. The grieving process was something I wanted and needed to understand so that I could help bring not only myself through it but also the children. I did a small word study on the word 'grief' in **Job 1:20** and from it learnt something very significant.

Job 1:20 *Job stood up and tore his robe in grief. Then he shaved his head and fell to the ground to worship. (NLT)*

grief - hurt, pain, vexation
     - God uses grief to shape, fashion, make, form, stretch into
      shape

What I came across through this word study was extremely helpful and showed me that grief is something that God is able to use to help shape and fashion us. It stretches us into shape and helps make and form us. I know that God has been shaping and fashioning me through grief. It hasn't been a process that started when Dorothy died but rather it was a process that started back in February 2012.

It was when Dorothy was diagnosed with a brain tumour and had to have surgery straight away that my grieving really started and the different stages of grief began to manifest themselves. When she was diagnosed and she told me via text while on the Year 12 camp, it was then that I developed a foggy mind and a cloudy head for about a period of three months. I started to withdraw almost immediately and there were elements of denial and isolation that started to take place in my life. Denial and isolation are quite often recognised as a part of the grieving process.

I pulled out of morning meetings at school because I didn't want people looking at me and pitying me and I honestly thought at that point Dorothy was in big trouble and wasn't going to live more than a few weeks. I didn't know if she would make it through the surgery. I was in a place of denial. This couldn't be happening to us and the physical symptoms continued to plague me. The cloudy head I was experiencing was really only relieved when I ran or played golf. The weight or the heaviness remained across my shoulders and the thought processes of, "This can't be happening to me." were very real. It took almost three months before the physical symptoms I was experiencing started to be alleviated. Running became my life line and as I started to become honest with myself about what was happening I started to turn to God for answers.

Many of the big questions started to come about in my life at this point (March 2012). Questions like, "Why is this happening to us? How could God allow this to happen to us? What have we done to deserve this? Where is God in all of this?" These were all questions that started to arise in my mind and they were directed at God. The story of Job was really the only thing I could hold onto through all of this. Verses that stood out to me in relation to my questions towards God were in **Job 13**.

Job 13:14-15 *Yes I will take my life in my hands and say what I really think. God might kill me but I have no other hope. I am going to argue my case with Him. (NLT)*

Anger and frustration are a widely recognised stage of the grieving process and something that I have had to deal with. I can still remember when I got given a red card while playing soccer. Around July 2013, I had been taking a lot of my anger out on the soccer pitch and over a few weeks I was becoming increasingly aggressive and would get angry and play hard.

When I was given the red card it was because there was a loose ball and an opposition player and myself were both running to get the ball. As we were going towards the ball the opposition player raised his arm and elbow towards me and so I went into protection mode and curled into a ball and hit him with my back to shield myself. He went down hard and I should have too but I didn't. First big mistake! Anyone who plays soccer knows you fall over. I remained standing and the opposition player wasn't happy so he jumped up, ran over and shoved me. Because I was walking towards him his push didn't affect me and I didn't really budge. Mistake number two! I should have fallen over. At this point I was very angry and shoved him back and of course he fell over. The referee pulled us over and proceeded to give the opposition player a yellow card and then said to me, "You can't retaliate like that!", and gave me a straight red and I had to leave the pitch.

Telling my family what happened when I got home and explaining to them how I did the wrong thing on the soccer pitch was a very hard thing. The children asked with big wide eyes, "What did you do daddy?" I proceeded to tell them and they were all in a state of shock, including Dorothy. Kelby - my youngest - who was nine at the time looked up at me and said, "Daddy you've brought shame on our family!" And you know what, he was absolutely right. I had to admit to them I had done exactly that. I had brought shame on our family. I had failed to do what I had been teaching them and therefore I had to be prepared to accept the consequences - a two week suspension.

It was during the following week that God really spoke to me while I was at school. I had a flow of thoughts best described as a still, small voice within; "Alistair, you have been taking your anger and frustration, over everything that has been happening with Dorothy, out on others on the soccer pitch. I don't want you to do this anymore. I want you to take your anger out on Me." This was an amazing word for me to receive because I had always been taught to behave respectfully and with a reverent attitude towards God, yet when I started to look at the Psalmists and how they poured out their heart to God I knew that this was what God wanted me to do. David in the Psalms didn't hold back and I wasn't going to anymore either. Anger was a very real part of the grief process in my life and God showed me how to deal with it. I learnt to call it 'honest prayer'. It is revealing my heart to God honestly. Being real! Venting my anger on God.

Another stage of grief that I have gone through over the last two years relates to bargaining and the 'what ifs'. For example, "Lord if You heal Dorothy I will serve you for the rest of my life." These types of thoughts happened more in 2012 than they did in the last eighteen months of Dorothy's life. In fact as I said in a previous chapter it was on the 10th of April 2014 that I stood beside Dorothy's grave (our twenty-first anniversary had she been alive) and resolved in my heart to serve God like never before.

The resolve and commitment in my heart to serve God was so strong and still is, and this is despite the fact that Dorothy has died. As I said at the celebration service, "God owes me nothing but I owe Him everything." God is still good even though Dorothy has left this life. My family is in God's hands. No lines have been drawn, no deals made. I have given my life to God regardless of the outcome. We are so grateful and thankful for our time with Dorothy and ultimately our future with her will be longer than the past we have spent with her - all eternity!

The 'what ifs' component of grief is where you ask the questions like: What if we had got a second opinion? What if we had gone to more healing meetings? What if we had stuck more stringently to a healthy diet? If only I had treated Dorothy more selflessly. This was an area that Dorothy and I both came to agreement on quite a number of months before she died. We recognised that through her suffering God had brought us closer together, He brought us closer to our children and more importantly He brought us closer to Himself. We had no regrets with the way we went about things. We both agreed if given the option of not going through this we wouldn't take it because the number of lives God has been able to minister to through one person's pain and suffering, including our own, is massive and the ripples still go on.

Dorothy is with God right now and I know, because of what God revealed to me and what she had said in the past to friends, that she is so pleased that she has been a part of what it took for setting the wheels in motion for me to seek God like never before. God has done things according to His plans and purposes, and more importantly in His timing. It hasn't been the suffering that has changed our lives but our response to suffering that has led to the change. In relation to the bargaining and 'what ifs' stage of grief it has been recognising God is with us and right there helping us every step of the way, regardless of the outcome, that really enabled us to stand strong.

Another stage of grief which the children and I were experiencing in the months after Dorothy's death related to sadness, sorrow and anguish. The sheer weight of the practical implications of dealing with death such as the celebration service, graveside service, obtaining a death certificate, filling in paperwork, getting names changed in house ownership, car ownership, putting the will in probate, closing bank accounts, working out finances, making superannuation claims and the like are all part of the process. They brought home strongly the fact that Dorothy had left this life.

The other key component in all of this, especially relating to sadness and sorrow, are the triggers day to day in relation to past memories. This is something you cannot escape from, but as I have alluded to previously, God had given the children and I keys to getting through this.

This was the biggest area of grief that the children and I were dealing with in those first six months and the passage of time was a key component to coming to terms with things. Instead of crying every day, as in the first two months, I would cry once every three days or so in the next few, but they were not tears of depression, rather they flowed from precious memories. The key for us continuing to work through all of this was recognising and receiving God's help day to day.

In a time of grief there will always be different views and voices as to how you should be handling it, but the one thing that is so important to me is that I do what God places in my heart and mind to do.

The Message Bible's introduction to Job articulates it beautifully where it brings out how the moment we find ourselves in a situation of any kind, people start showing up to let us know exactly what is wrong with us and what we must do to get better. At first we are impressed that they bother with us and are amazed with their answers. It all sounds so hopeful but then we begin to wonder why is it that for all their apparent compassion we feel worse instead of better after they have said their piece? Answers are not rejected in Job but rather answers severed from the Source, that is the living God, are those which are rejected. We cannot have answers or receive them if they are severed from the heart and mind of God.

Another significant part of the grieving process was acceptance, that is, acceptance that Dorothy had left this life. It was not a period of happiness nor was it a period of depression. It was acceptance of the fact that Dorothy was no longer here with us. For me this was something that I have been able to accept possibly a little more readily than many people who go through the death of a loved one, because of the fact that God used me to speak to Dorothy in such a powerful way in the final moments of her life on this earth. To communicate to her on God's behalf, "Well done good and faithful servant. Enter into the joy of the Lord." and then to witness her breathe her last and leave this life makes the acceptance of her death possible.

To know beyond a shadow of a doubt that Dorothy is in heaven, that she has passed from this life to the next, was and still is such a blessing. I am at peace with the fact that she has gone. There is still the sadness that she is no longer with me and that I can no longer experience life with her but God is still with me and the children, giving us the strength we need.

The Biblical reality is that it is normal to hurt and it is necessary to grieve. It is moving from denial and isolation to personal honesty. It is moving from anger and frustration to honesty with God. From bargaining and 'what ifs' to asking God for help with what we are going through right now. From anguish, sorrow and sadness to receiving God's help daily. And it is accepting the reality that Dorothy has gone and recognising that we will see her again one day.

I didn't have it all together back in those early months, far from it, nor do I have it together now, but I do know this, God has shaped and fashioned the children and I through grief and we are stronger today than we were yesterday. I know that I am growing spiritually stronger by the day and all I want to do is pursue God more and more. A new chapter has opened in our lives and we move forward with faith, hope and love in our hearts.

Philippians 3:8 *Yes everything else is worthless when compared to the infinite value of knowing Christ Jesus my Lord. For His sake I have discarded everything else, counting it all as garbage, so that I could gain Christ and become one with Him.* (NLT)

Nothing compares to the infinite value of knowing Christ Jesus!

Chapter 26: Diligently Seeking God

A passage that really became important to me about five months on from Dorothy's death was **Hebrews 11:5-6**.

Hebrews 11:5-6 *By faith Enoch was taken away so that he did not see death, 'and was not found, because God had taken him'; for before he was taken he had this testimony, that he pleased God. But without faith it is impossible to please Him, for he who comes to God must believe that He is, and that He is a rewarder of those who diligently seek Him. (NKJV)*

This passage really came alive to me during this time because even in the midst of going through grief I was seeking Him. It states that God is a rewarder of those who diligently seek Him. This is a reality that I have found to be completely true since November 2012 as I have sought after God.

Enoch was a man who pleased God. He had this testimony that he pleased God and then the verse goes on to show us how he pleased God. He had faith first of all to believe that God is, that is, God exists. In other words it was through his belief in God's existence that Enoch pleased God, but that was just the starting point. He also believed that God was a rewarder of those who diligently sought Him and Enoch got the ultimate reward as a result of His faith and diligently seeking Him - God took him.

Today I personally believe that 'God is', and because I believe that 'He is' and that He sent His Son, Jesus, to die and pay the price for my sin I have received God's unmerited favour. This places me in a position of right standing before Him so that I can have a relationship with Him. It is not by any work but it is purely by faith that I have come into this position. It is a part of God's grace. The second thing which is significant is that God has rewarded me as I have diligently sought Him.

What does He reward us with? So many times, as Christians, it is possible to believe that the reward for seeking God is prosperity, wealth, happiness and well-being. If we seek God and follow after Him, He will reward us with these things on earth. The problem with this line of thinking is that when trials and adversity come, people can blame God because He isn't delivering His end of the bargain or more to the point, what they believe to be the bargain - He isn't rewarding them the way they think He should, for seeking Him. People fail to recognise that the reward for diligently seeking God is God revealing more of Himself.

James 4:8 *Draw near to God and He will draw near to you. (NKJV)*

I know that because of the trials and suffering that my family and I have had to go through we have sought after God like never before. Yes Dorothy has left this life but the reward of knowing God so much more through all of this is undeniable. Both Dorothy and I declared while she was still alive that even if we could go back and change what we've been through we would choose not to. Why? Because through the pain and through the suffering God has brought us closer to Himself; He brought us closer to each other and He brought us closer together as a family.

Dorothy is no longer with us, she is in heaven, but the ripples of her life have caused me to have a level of faith in God that He exists, and that He is rewarder of those who diligently seek Him. I am experiencing firsthand the reward of knowing Him in a far greater depth and dimension than ever before. It is my experience that you cannot spend 2-3 hours a day seeking God and not be changed. The amazing thing in all of this is there is no place I would rather be. The more time I spend with Him the more He reveals of Himself! Moses knew firsthand the reward of diligently seeking God. In **Exodus 33** God tells Moses to go and take the Promised Land and He would send His Angel before them. However, He (God) would not go up in their midst lest He consume them for they were a stiff necked people. Moses' response was amazing.

Exodus 33:18 *Then he said to Him, "If Your Presence does not go with us, do not bring us up from here." (NKJV)*

Moses was not interested in going anywhere without God and because of this he found grace in God's sight. As a result of finding grace in God's sight Moses' response was, "Please show me Your glory." He wanted more of God.

I do not want to go through this life unless God is with me. I have received and continue to receive the reward of diligently seeking Him and that is a greater level of knowing Him than I ever thought possible. I have a peace with God that cannot be explained, but is definitely being experienced day to day even though Dorothy has left this life. Death is merely a transition from this life into eternity and I know as long as I draw breath I will continue to diligently seek Him.

I watched a movie during this time called Soul Surfer which is based on a true story about Bethany Hamilton who lost her arm due to a shark attack. Something Bethany said really confirmed what we had experienced. She said, *"I wouldn't change what happened to me because then I wouldn't have the chance in front of all of you, to embrace more people than I ever could have with two arms."*

The movie showed how she asked the big questions of God like, "Why did He let this happen to me? How can going through this work together for good?" I too have asked many questions of God but the facts are undeniable. The ripples of Dorothy's life have led to myself and so many others diligently seeking God more than ever before. The reward for this is to know Him more whether it be in this life or the next! I often wonder would I have embraced God to the extent that I have today if Dorothy and I hadn't gone through these difficult times? I think not!

Does a person have to go through experiences like this to start diligently seeking God? I don't believe so. I believe it is possible to learn from the experiences of others. I have been saying for a while now, "Would I wish what Dorothy and I went through on anyone else? No way! But do I wish that others could learn from our experience? Absolutely!" It is my hope and prayer that you can take what we have learnt from our experiences and apply these truths to your lives so that you may be rewarded with more of Him as you diligently seek Him.

Chapter 27: Is God With Us?

After Dorothy's death there were a lot of adjustments that the children and I needed to make; providing the children with opportunities to share where they were at and how things were going became a monthly ritual. They learnt very quickly that when I said we were going to Sofia's (a local restaurant) that it was 'talk' time and even though they would pretend to moan and groan they would still open up and walk away from the experience feeling that they had been listened to and had a voice.

I vividly remember taking the children out for a meal at Sofia's a number of months after Dorothy's passing and I once again gave them an opportunity to share how things were going. Kelby revealed that he had been coping well and had not really been crying much at all anymore. He still had moments of sadness but he didn't stay in that place for too long and what was really encouraging was his love tank was being filled by hugs from teachers and friends which was wonderful to know because it meant that he was feeling the love and support of people he saw each day. This really was so important for him and he still considered me to be his favourite person which was really special!

Kalani was also holding up quite well and not crying or getting upset in relation to Dorothy as much. She, like Kelby, had moments of sadness but her view, which she articulated really well, was that if mum were still alive she would be in even more pain but now she is in a far better place, safe in God's hands. Kalani's faith is strong and this is clearly evident by the way she engages at church and the devotions she shares with us around the meal table. She loves working through her devotional books. She is being well supported by family, close family friends, school friends and her teachers at school. What I am really grateful for is the fact that she is willing to open up and share with me about personal things confronting her.

At this point I was thinking this is great - two children down and things are going well - and then it was Jayden's turn! He was brutally honest and said some things I needed to hear. In his own way he said that he had been struggling more and crying more than he had at the start. His issue had been adjusting to differences between Dorothy and me in terms of parenting - smack one - straight between the eyes! He explained that I follow through a lot more and have a tougher edge, whereas with mum he could sit down and discuss things more openly and be hugged and comforted. She would be a lot more understanding whereas I would probably say, "Toughen up Princess!"

He then went on to say that he trusted mum more than he did me - smack two - straight between the eyes! He is definitely far more sensitive than the other two children and he was struggling more than them. I learnt that I needed to continue talking with him one on one and really take the time to listen to him. When Dorothy was there we balanced one another out but now because it is just me it has become apparent that it was necessary for me to soften my approach and be far more sensitive, which I must admit took a little bit of effort!

I clearly need the sensitivity of the Holy Spirit in working with the children. I lacked Dorothy's sensitivity but with the Holy Spirit leading me and guiding me all things are possible and hopefully the way I parent has improved as a result.

In the midst of all this we knew that God was with us and the ways in which He showed us this have been quite amazing. I definitely no longer believe in 'random' but rather I believe in 'divine appointments' as a result of things that happened. I seem to go these days from one divine appointment to another.

I remember when the Tarago's automatic transmission failed and we were driving around in our Pajero, which we were trying to sell as we no longer needed two cars. Basically to get a reconditioned automatic transmission put in we were looking at $3500 but fortunately the people doing the job were able to locate a second hand transmission from a Tarago that had only done 110,000 kilometres and they could fit it for $1700. This was great in itself but then after giving the go ahead for the repair the very next day I received in the bank account a reconciliation payment from Family Assistance for $1715! I had no idea the payment was coming and I just said, "Thankyou Lord - perfect timing!"

The following night a man came to the door collecting for Peter Mac (Cancer research) and started to share about how cancer affects so many people today and he shared about his own father's experience of cancer and I was able to empathise with him. I then felt prompted to share with Him about Dorothy's departure from this life and I used the opportunity to share about how God spoke through me to speak those final amazing words Dorothy heard in this life, "Well done good and faithful servant. Enter into the joy of the Lord." He was touched and his final words were, "I have had many conversations tonight but yours was definitely the most different!"

In relation to the selling of the Pajero I had another divine appointment after the Tarago had been fixed. Jayden had a birthday party over in Plenty, which was a sleep over, and I had to drive him over there on a Saturday around 1 pm. Just before going there I got a missed phone call notification. It was the second time a person had tried to call me so I called him back. He was very keen to look at the Pajero but he lived in Melton. I couldn't see him Saturday but I mentioned that I would be going to pick up Jayden near Plenty and we could meet near there. He liked that idea and so we arranged to meet at the Eltham Soccer ground at 10:15 am. This man arrived with his wife around 10:10 am, five minutes after us. I got out, introduced myself and then proceeded to tell him about the car. He walked around the car once and said the Pajero was what he was looking for. I asked him if he wanted to test drive it first, but he figured that because I was willing to drive it from my home to

Eltham (a thirty-five minute drive) it couldn't be that bad! I then proceeded to show him everything, including the paint work issues. I told him about the smoke blowing issues and how we used a thicker oil to curb the problem. In spite of these things I was able to say that overall it was a good reliable car. He was still quite keen to buy the car even after me telling him all of the car's problems!

I offered him the option of coming out to the school in the next week, which would be closer for him, but he surprised me by saying they would prefer to follow us home that day and take the car straight away - they would pay cash! So that's what we did. We drove home, the children emptied out the car and I signed off on the paper work. We then proceeded to have a chat before they went. It was during this time that the Holy Spirit opened up the perfect opportunity to share the story about Dorothy's final moments to them and they were quite impacted by it. They had lost their son some seven years earlier which they didn't really go into detail about, but it was something they lived with every day. They were a wonderful couple and I really believe God was able to use this divine appointment to impact on their lives. This was another ripple flowing out from Dorothy's life.

The amazing thing about the sale itself was they were happy to pay the asking price of $3000. They gave me too much money initially. I gave them back $50 as they had given me $3050! I know beyond a shadow of a doubt that God was in this and that He orchestrated everything according to His plans and purposes. I really do thank God for giving us a fair price for the car as well as really blessing the couple who bought the car.

Although these are just a few examples I can honestly answer the question, "Is God with us? Definitely!"

Chapter 28: God's Grace

One of the things that has become very apparent to me as I have spent time diligently seeking God throughout this period of suffering and grief is the grace of God and the threefold nature to it, that is, past, present and future. His grace first of all brings us to a position of right standing with Him and completely deals with our <u>past</u>. His grace then also allows us to live our life in the present. By His grace we can live a life of holiness without having to try and strive to do so. As we come closer and closer to Him by diligently seeking Him, the way we think, feel and act becomes wholly conformed to that which is in His heart and mind. It is only through relationship, that these things become a reality in our <u>present</u> day life. In other words out of diligently seeking God flows His divine enablement (His grace) to live a holy and righteous life. In the present, right now, we are able to live, not according to our own selfish nature, but according to God's divine nature. He has given us everything we need for living a godly life.

2 Peter 1:2-4 *May God give you, more and more grace as you grow in your knowledge of God and Jesus our Lord. By His divine power, God has given us everything we need for living a godly life. We have received all of this by coming to know Him, the one who called us to Himself by means of His marvellous glory and excellence. And because of His glory and excellence He has given us great and precious promises. These are the promises that enable you to share His divine nature and escape the world's corruptions caused by human desires. (NLT)*

The final part to God's grace is that He gives us the divine enablement by the Holy Spirit dwelling in us to do that which He calls us to do day by day both now and in the <u>future</u>. I have everything I need to be able to fulfil all that God is asking of me now and in the days ahead. He is with me and His grace flows as I walk in obedience to His leading and guiding and that can only happen as I diligently seek Him and continually walk in close fellowship with

Him. God is starting to show me more and more of the exceeding riches of His grace in His kindness towards us in Christ Jesus.

Ephesians 2:4-10 *But God who is rich in mercy, because of His great love with which He loved us, even when we were dead in trespasses, made us alive together with Christ (by grace you have been saved), and raised us up together, and made us sit together in the heavenly places in Christ Jesus, that in the ages to come He might show the exceeding riches of His grace in His kindness towards us in Christ Jesus. For by grace you have been saved through faith, and that not of yourselves; it is the gift of God, not of works, lest anyone should boast. For we are His workmanship, created in Christ Jesus for good works, which God prepared beforehand that we should walk in them. (NKJV)*

As another close friend shared with me, grace is God's generosity to us. Once again grace brings us to a position of right standing with God and then also gives us the ability to live the way He wants us to live and do the things He wants us to do. By grace we have been saved, by grace we are able to live a holy and righteous life and by grace we are able to do the things He would have us do.

How do we appropriate His grace? It is one thing to hear these things but it is another thing to walk in it. Many people struggle to live according to this truth and to appropriate God's word to us. Yes by grace we have been saved, yes by His grace we have received God's enablement to live a holy life and yes by His grace we are able to do the things He would have us do in the future. But why is it that so many Christians struggle to walk in this truth?

I believe it all ties back to **Hebrews 11:6**.

Hebrews 11:6 *But without faith it is impossible to please Him, for he who comes to God must believe that He is, and that He is a rewarder of those who diligently seek Him. (NKJV)*

We appropriate His grace in our lives by diligently seeking Him. God's grace is released in our lives and is given to us as we walk in close fellowship with Him.

The fact is Christians come to a position of right standing with God because they believe that 'He is', but the way to grow in grace and peace is to know Him. How do you come to a place of knowing Him? You have to diligently seek Him. That is when the reward comes - more of Him. The more you have of Him the less the things of this world appeal to you. God's divine enablement to live the way He wants you to live is released.

Chapter 29: It Is Well With My Soul

The children and I were strengthened a lot around eight months after Dorothy's passing, particularly by the words of a song that a friend from work, Lucille, passed onto me. The song was called 'It is well' by Kristine Dimarco and it has become very meaningful for my family. Some key words of the song are:

> Through it all my eyes are on You and it is well with me
> So let go my soul and trust in Him
> It is well with my soul

It is very similar in focus to a famous hymn 'It is well with my soul' written by Horatio Spafford.

> When peace, like a river, attendeth my way,
> When sorrows like sea billows roll;
> Whatever my lot, Thou hast taught me to say,
> It is well, it is well with my soul.

These words have really ministered to us as a family and, even in the midst of everything the children and I have gone through, it is well with our soul. The words of the original hymn by Horatio Spafford were written in the 1870s. He was a very wealthy business man and had five children. He lost a son at the young age of four to scarlet fever and he also lost a lot of property as a result of the Great Chicago Fires at a similar time and then because of these tough times he decided to go on vacation with his family. He ended up not being able to go at the same time as his family because of urgent business that came up, so he sent his wife and four daughters on ahead of him by ship to go to Europe where he was going to meet up with them later. He then found out via a cabled message from his wife that because of a collision the ship they were sailing on sank and only his wife survived. The message she sent said, "Saved Alone". As Horatio was sailing to meet up with his wife in England the captain pulled him aside at the point where the ship his family had been on sank and in response he went to his cabin and penned the hymn, 'It is well with my soul' .

This song has blessed thousands of people who have found comfort in the words he wrote. I too am one who has found comfort in them because the truth of these words has become a reality in my life. Through it all, that is through everything that I have gone through with Dorothy, it is well with my soul. My eyes have been on God and it is well with me. It has taken me a while to get to this point, of saying it is well with my soul, but I can now and that is regardless of all that has happened to us. God is with the children and myself in the midst of our suffering and grief.

Psalm 40:1-3 *I waited patiently for the Lord to help me, and He turned to me and heard my cry. He lifted me out of the pit of despair, out of the mud and mire. He set my feet on solid ground, and steadied me as I walked along. He has given me a new song to sing, a hymn of praise to our God. Many will see what He has done and be amazed. They will put their trust in the Lord. (NLT)*

I believe this passage reflects what God has done in our lives. We fell face down in the mud and there were those around about whom God used to help lift us out of the mud. We have been taken from the mud and mire and He has set our feet on solid ground and steadied us as we have walked along. He has placed a new song in our heart and many people have seen this and been amazed. Others are putting their trust in God because the evidence of what He has done in our lives is there for all to see.

2 Corinthians 12:9 *And He said to me, "My grace is sufficient for you, for My strength is made perfect in weakness. Therefore most gladly I will rather boast in my infirmities, that the power of Christ may rest upon me." (NKJV)*

God has really done a work of confirmation in our hearts in relation to this song. The words have been a real source of encouragement and strength. Everything I have gone through in relation to Dorothy over the last couple of years has brought me into a place of diligently seeking God like never before. My eyes are upon Him and have been upon Him through it all and I now have this real sense that it is well with my soul.

The amazing thing was that I received a message from another friend, Danielle, via Facebook, exactly one week after I had received the song from Lucille. She said that in her quiet time with God, God had impressed to her to send me a song. She prayed that God would speak to me through this song and it was the exact same song Lucille had sent! This was an awesome confirmation of what God had been saying to me and to the children. It was now through two people that God had sealed this in my heart. It is well with my soul and I will continue to press into God like never before. No matter what continues to come my way my heart is for God with my eyes on Him. I know no matter what happens we will be okay because God is with us.

What does it mean to say, "It is well with my soul?" I found this quote by Eric Jonas Swenson which was very meaningful to me.

The peace Jesus gives doesn't depend on conditions or circumstances. It comes from knowing you're God's child and that your heavenly Father controls the universe, loves you and always has your best interests at heart. That's why people who've lost everything will often tell you they wouldn't trade what they've learned, even it meant recouping all their losses.

The peace Jesus gives brings a sense of assurance that no matter what happens to you, "It is well with my soul."

John 14:27 *Peace I leave with you My peace I give to you; not as the world gives do I give to you. Let not your heart be troubled, neither let it be afraid. (NKJV)*

Another thing that I believe God placed on my heart in relation to the children is found in **Psalm 127:3-5**.

Psalm 127:3-5 *Children are a gift from the Lord; they are a reward from Him. Children born to a young man are like arrows in a warrior's hands. How joyful is the man whose quiver is full of them! He will not be put to shame when he confronts his accusers at the city gates. (NLT)*

Children are a heritage from the Lord. They are a good gift, as arrows are in the hand of a mighty man. With prudence they may be directed towards the mark, God's glory and service to their generation. I will pursue God no matter what comes my way. My care is to keep myself in the love of God, a giving, sacrificial love with no expectation of return. My children are a heritage from the Lord, arrows in my hand and while I have them in my quiver I will train them and direct them towards the mark, that is, God's glory and service to their generation. After they have left my hand I have to trust and hold onto the belief that the training of their heart and God's leading will hold them in good stead for life.

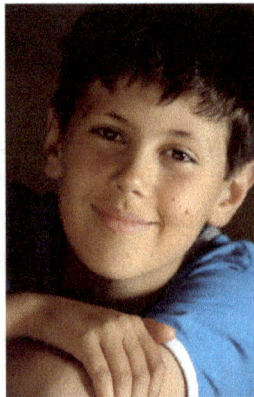

Chapter 30: Our Position Today – The Promise Received

As I was on a run towards the end of December 2014 the first thing that came to me was a memory of a message I received on the morning of the celebration service for Dorothy. I was somewhat stressed and a close friend sent me a text that was spot on and what I needed to hear.

Text Received: *Hi Alistair, You are going to hold many different positions/roles today ... husband, father, brother, son in law, team mate, friend, teacher, colleague, uncle, etc, etc. Most of these will demand much from you emotionally, spiritually, socially, physically. As you hold these positions and juggle the demands for each I pray you would know the most important position you hold today is as God's beloved, treasured son. I pray that you would know this position demands nothing ... except remaining in Him. May you experience His protection, security, peace as He hides you under the shadow of His wings on this really difficult day. Have been and will be praying.*

The reason I believe God brought this text message back to me is because He wanted to show me that this word is just as true today as it was back then for the celebration service. Every single day of my life I will hold different roles and functions and they will demand much from me but the most important thing is that I know that I am God's beloved, treasured son and this position demands nothing except remaining in Him. Why is it so important that I remain in Him? Because He can then give me everything I need to face all of those different roles/functions. I will experience His protection, security and peace as He hides me under the shadows of His wings.

Psalm 91:1-4 *He who dwells in the secret place of the Most High shall abide under the shadow of the Almighty. I will say of the Lord, "He is my refuge and my fortress; My God in Him I will trust." Surely He shall deliver you from the snare of the fowler and from the* *perilous pestilence. He shall cover you with His feathers, And under His wings you shall take refuge; His truth shall be your shield and buckler. (NKJV)*

The truth that God reveals to me each day is my shield. It is what I use to fend off blows of the enemy.

The 'Edenic' covenant (God's first covenant with mankind) declared God's creative purpose for mankind, including covenantal relationship with Himself, character, dominion, fruitfulness and eternal life upon obedience and faith. I believe that God's original, creative purpose for Adam, Eve and all mankind was relationship with Himself and the whole redemptive story is all about restoring mankind to that place of relationship with Him.

Once again the most important truth that God has revealed to me in recent times is based around **Hebrews 11:5-6**.

Hebrews 11:5-6 *By faith Enoch was taken away so that He did not see death, "and was not found, because God had taken him"; for before he was taken he had this testimony, that he pleased God. But without faith it is impossible to please Him, for he who comes to God must believe that He is, and that He is a rewarder of those who diligently seek Him. (NKJV)*

I believe with everything within me that God is a rewarder of those who diligently seek Him. It is not a reward of health, prosperity and riches in this life. To me it is not even a reward of mansions in heaven or heaven itself. I believe the reward itself is knowing Him. The more you get to know Him, the more you want to know Him! I don't seek God to achieve my own goals or purposes but I seek Him because I just want to know Him.

Luke 12:21 *Yes a person is a fool to store up earthly wealth but not have a rich relationship with God. (NLT)*

I have taken this to heart and I have diligently sought God like never before since November 2012. My faith has grown in this time and something I have learnt is that everyone is given an initial measure of faith and that is different for every single person. We all start at different places or stages when we become Christians, depending on our background and upbringing but it is not to stop there.

Romans 12:3-6 *For I say through the grace given to me, to everyone who is among you not to think of himself more highly than he ought to think, but to think soberly, as God has given to each one a measure of faith. For as we have many members in one body, but all members do not have the same function so we being many are one body in Christ, and individually members of one another. Having then gifts differing according to the grace that is given to us, let us use them: if prophecy, let us prophesy in proportion to our faith; (NKJV)*

We have all been dealt a measure of faith and we are to act and move in proportion to our faith, however it is possible to grow in our faith. Our faith can grow exceedingly.

2 Thessalonians 1:3 *We are bound to thank God always for you, brethren, as it is fitting, because your faith grows exceedingly, and the love of everyone of you all abounds towards each other. (NKJV)*

We all have a starting point and it can be very different from someone else but everyone of us can grow in our faith. How does that happen?

Romans 10:17 *So then faith comes by hearing, and hearing by the word of God. (NKJV)*

It is hearing God's living, quickened word to us each day that causes our faith to grow. What is faith? Faith is a persuasion, a conviction, an absolute inward certainty that something is true. It is a power that seizes upon the soul. We don't know how we know something is true. We just know! The important provision here is that the word given or received can never contradict God's written word - The Bible.

That which was given initially, has been added to and has increased above the degree originally given, is what it means for our faith to grow exceedingly. Has my faith grown in the last two years? I believe that it has increased exceedingly beyond the measure I began with, as I have on a daily basis received God's living word to me. As I hear from God faith comes and the power of His grace, that is, His divine enablement is released within me to be able to apply, and walk in, that which He shows me.

What does diligently seeking God look like in my life? If I had to explain to someone how I diligently seek God what would I say? The answer for me is found in **Isaiah 50:4**.

Isaiah 50:4 *The Sovereign LORD has given me His words of wisdom, so that I know how to comfort the weary. Morning by morning he wakens me and opens my understanding to his will. (NLT)*

This has been my reality since November 2012. God has woken me each morning and I have gone to my secret place which is my office in the early hours of the morning and I have learnt to sit and wait upon Him.

Matthew 6:6 *"But you when you pray, go into your room, and when you have shut your door, pray to your Father who is in the secret place; and your Father who sees in secret will reward you openly. (NKJV)*

In all of this I desire to inspire others to come to God and to help them draw into greater depths and dimensions in God. I want people to know and understand that they can learn to hear His voice and understand His heart and mind. I desire for them to learn to walk in obedience to what He shows them without having to strive to do so. The fact is, as we diligently seek God day after day, the way we think, feel and act starts to become more and more conformed to the heart and mind of God. Righteous living becomes a reality as the Holy Spirit works in us.

What is the lowest possible benchmark that I believe, in terms of our position in God, is now obtainable for us in the kingdom of heaven? I believe it is the great cloud of witnesses that provide some of the examples of the lowest possible bench marks. People like Enoch, Noah, Abraham and Moses. How can I say this? I can say this because these men, with the exception of Enoch who was taken, died in faith not having received the promises.

Hebrews 11:13 *These all died in faith, not having received the promises, but having seen them from afar off were assured of them, embraced them and confessed that they were strangers and pilgrims on the earth. (NKJV)*

Hebrews 11:39 *And all these, having obtained a good testimony through faith, did not receive the promise, God having provided something better for us, that they should not be made perfect apart from us. (NKJV)*

We today have received the promises. We have received Jesus and the Holy Spirit. We have an amazing <u>position</u> compared to them. All who enter into the New Covenant today are in this position.

Luke 24:49 *Behold I send the <u>Promise</u> of My Father upon you; but tarry in the city of Jerusalem until you are endued with power from on high. (NKJV)*

2 Peter 1:3-4 *By His divine power, God has given us <u>everything we need for living a godly life</u>. We have received all this by coming to <u>know</u> Him, the one who called us to Himself by means of His marvellous glory and excellence. And because of His glory and excellence, He has given us great and precious <u>promises</u>. These are*

His <u>promises</u> that enable you to share His divine nature and escape the world's corruption caused by human desires. (NLT)

Acts 2:38-39 *Then Peter said to them, "Repent and let everyone of you be baptised in the name of Jesus Christ for the remission of sins; and you shall receive the gift of the Holy Spirit for the <u>promise</u> is to you and your children, and to all who are afar off, as many as the Lord our God will call." (NKJV)*

The position we have in Christ today is amazing but do we truly walk in the strength of that position? Or do we settle for a life that is far less than what was intended? If there is still any doubt as to whether the men listed above are possible low bench marks then read the words Jesus spoke.

Matthew 11:11-14 *Assuredly I say to you, among those born of women there has not risen one greater than John the Baptist; but he who is least in the kingdom of heaven is greater than he. And from the days of John the Baptist until now the kingdom of heaven suffers violence, and the violent take it by force. For all the prophets and the laws prophesied until John. And if you are willing to receive it, he is Elijah who is to come.(NKJV)*

Luke 7:28 *For I say unto you among those born of women there is not a greater prophet than John the Baptist; but he who is least in the kingdom of heaven is greater than he. (NKJV)*

Of all the men born of a woman John the Baptist was the greatest but then Jesus states that he who is least in the kingdom of God is greater than him. How do we come to this <u>position</u> of being one of the least in the kingdom of heaven yet still being greater than John the Baptist or others born of women before him like Enoch, Noah, Abraham and Moses?

Romans 10:8-10 *But what does it say? "The word is near you, on your mouth and in your heart" (that is the word of faith which we* *preach): that if you confess with your mouth the Lord Jesus and believe in your heart that God has raised Him from the dead, you will be saved. For with the heart one believes unto righteousness, and with the mouth confession is made unto salvation. (NKJV)*

It is when we confess with our mouth the Lord Jesus and believe in our heart that God has raised Him from the dead we will be saved. The Holy Spirit then comes and dwells in us but it is vital that we experience His inspiration and impulse in our life. In other words we need to be filled with the Spirit.

Everything that Jesus did while He lived His life on this earth flowed out of His relationship with the Father. His example is the way God desires it to be with us. Knowing God and knowing that I am His treasured son is the most important position I hold and out of that flows all of the things He would have me do. That is what matters.

Matthew 7:21-23 *Not everyone who says to me, "Lord, Lord," shall enter the kingdom of heaven, but he who does the will of My Father in heaven. Many will say to me in that day, "Lord, Lord, have we not prophesied in Your name, and done many wonders in Your name?" And then I will declare to them "I never <u>knew</u> you; depart from Me, you who practice lawlessness." (NKJV)*

The key to living this life is <u>knowing</u> Him and doing what He shows us to do. In order for that to happen we have to be able to hear from God. As we hear from God and obey, we can do great works and even greater works than Jesus can be done by us because He has gone to the Father.

John 14:11-14 *Believe Me that I am in the Father and the Father is in Me, or else believe Me for the sake of the works themselves. Most assuredly I say to you, he who believes in Me, the works that I do he will do also and greater works than these he will do, because I go to My Father. (NKJV)*

As I look at these passages I am inspired by the thought that God wants us to diligently seek Him so that we can know Him. That is the reward and as a result of knowing Him, He can use our lives to draw others to Him that they might also come to know Him to a degree that they never thought possible. The great men of faith who have gone before us are to me the lowest possible benchmarks of knowing God because we have received the Promise! We have the Holy Spirit residing in us and He is able to teach, lead and guide us day to day. Jesus lived a life dependent upon the Father. How much more should we?

John 14:26 *But the Helper, the Holy Spirit, whom the Father will send in My name, He will teach you all things, and bring to your remembrance all things that I said to you. (NKJV)*

Our lives are a Christ-like fragrance rising up to God as we live diligently seeking Him. This is what it means to live a life that is pleasing to God. The fragrance of my life is going to be perceived differently by others depending on where they are at. To those who are being saved, the fragrance of my life is going to be a life giving perfume, but to those who are perishing I will be a dreadful smell of death and doom.

2 Corinthians 2:14-16 *Now thank God! He has made us His captives and continues to lead us along in Christ's triumphal procession. Now He uses us to spread the knowledge of Christ everywhere, like a sweet perfume. Our lives are a Christ-like fragrance rising up to God. But this fragrance is perceived differently by those who are being saved and by those who are perishing. To those who are perishing we are a dreadful smell of death and doom. But to those who are being saved, we are a life giving perfume. And who is adequate for such a task as this? (NLT)*

If we ask the Father to grow in a deeper relationship with Him, will He give us a stone or a serpent? No, I believe He will reveal Himself to us.

Matthew 7:7-10 *Ask, and it will be given to you; seek, and you will find; knock and it will be opened to you. For everyone who asks receives, and he who seeks finds, and to him who knocks it will be opened. Or what man is there among you who, if his son asks for bread, will give him a stone? Or if he asks for a fish will give him a serpent? If you then being evil, know how to give good gifts to your children, how much more will your Father in heaven give good things to those who ask Him! (NKJV)*

If a person is willing to pursue God and they are asking, seeking and knocking they will receive, find and have the door opened to them. Why? Because we serve a loving God who is our heavenly Father, who knows how to give good things to His children who ask Him.

God will reveal Himself to those who willingly choose to seek Him. Just as with Moses, God speaks when He sees that we have turned aside.

Exodus 3:4 *So when the Lord saw that he turned aside to look, God called to him from the midst of the bush and said, "Moses, Moses!" And he said, "Here I am." (NKJV)*

He draws near as we draw near to Him. The critical thing is diligently seeking Him, just as Jesus often withdrew to spend time alone with the Father.

James 4:8 *Draw near to God and He will draw near to you. Cleanse your hands, you sinners; and purify your hearts, you double-minded. (NKJV)*

The best thing that God can give us is more of Himself. That is the reward. The more He reveals of Himself the more I want to know Him. I have no desire to be great but I do desire to know how great He is and that others might also realise that knowing Him is the ultimate reward!

I think all of this is beautifully summed up in some words I heard spoken at church. *The essence of Christianity is to know God and make God known.* This is truly the reality of my life now. All of these things have come from going through suffering, pain and grief. To know God in the midst of all this is more precious than I can ever say in words.

Chapter 31: Making The Most Of Every Opportunity

To know God is the most important part of my life and as I have continued to diligently seek Him day by day He has rewarded me by revealing more and more of Himself to me. As a result of this the opportunities to make God known to others has become a frequent occurrence. To share of God's grace in the midst of suffering and grief has been a privilege, as I experienced with a neighbour who lives across the road.

The conversation I had with her was not what I was expecting or what I would do at all normally. I was whipper snipping the front lawn and I saw this neighbour across the road and waved to her. I hadn't seen her for a long time and she was out doing some gardening. I continued on with my whipper snipping and as I did I experienced a flow of thoughts saying, "Go speak to her, go speak to her." My first thought was I really needed to get the whipper snipping done but the flow of thoughts continued! She was near to her front porch and so I went over the road and up to her brick fence and called out to her.

My neighbour came over and I asked her how she was going and it became apparent very quickly that she was not in a great place. She was visibly upset and I asked if she was all right. She told me her husband had died on Thursday, three days before I spoke to her! I had no idea whatsoever and so I then just started to chat with her and talk to her about what had happened. I listened and let her talk and she clearly needed to do this. Basically he had been diagnosed with pancreatic cancer back in July 2014 and in a matter of three months he had deteriorated very quickly and wasted away to skin and bone. She had taken 'carers leave' to look after him, as well as some annual leave. He died in October 2014.

After telling her story for about half an hour, she inquired after Dorothy. She had last seen Dorothy in February 2014 at the train station. I had to fill her in on Dorothy's passing and she was a little shocked. I talked about our faith and what we held onto, as well as how we have been dealing with things since. One thing that came out was that she had turned to God through all of this, and her family had as well. The level and depth of conversation I was able to have with her was significant because I was able to understand what she had been going through. By the time we had wrapped up our conversation which was probably about one and a half hours, she had unpacked and unloaded to someone who was really able to sympathise with her.

I think it is absolutely amazing that the very person who comes across her path at that moment in time had an understanding of what she was going through because he had just gone through it. We were both able to relate and share stories and it was a very powerful time. I could easily have missed this opportunity, if I had not responded to the inward flow of thoughts that came to me.

A follow up conversation to this one, occurred a couple of months later as the children and I were preparing to go to church for the 5.00 pm service in Dec 2014. As we were getting into the car I saw this same neighbour and I went over for a quick chat which ended up going for a little longer than expected! The conversation we had was very thought provoking and the connection we had because we had both lost a loved one continued. To put this conversation in perspective this neighbour was age twenty when she got married and had been married for forty-seven years when her husband died.

We both shared honestly with one another as to where we were at and I truly believe that it was another divine appointment. One thing that came out which was of particular significance was she had met a man, that she hadn't seen for twenty years, at her husband's funeral and then she saw him again at another funeral some three weeks later. They had struck up a friendship but her family were quick to criticise the fact that she was spending time with someone else so soon after just losing her husband. I have learnt because of my experience not to judge people in this situation because I know how tough those first two months are.

My neighbour shared how she was missing her husband and although she would go out to have 'breakfast with him' and 'talk with him' she wasn't really coping with him being gone. She revealed how big the void in her life was as a result of him not being there and how friends that she had known before were no longer catching up with her because they felt awkward talking to her. I could really relate to everything she was saying and given my experience at around the two month mark after Dorothy's passing I could relate to what she was going through.

As I outlined previously, it was at that time I was missing the depth of Dorothy's love for me the most and I missed the intimacy of not being able to share and unpack things with Dorothy every day. I felt that I no longer had the freedom to open up my heart to some of my close friends who had supported me before Dorothy died. People with good intentions and hearts of concern actually made things tougher for me.

Not to be able to unpack and share things with someone you have spent the last twenty years with is unbelievably hard and I fully understand why people in this situation look for someone else with whom to share what they are going through. I can also understand the care and concern of others who are worried for your well-being and want to protect you from entering into a friendship that could lead to further hurt and pain.

This really revealed to me how significant the touch I received from the Holy Spirit was. When he 'blanketed' me after a run from one end of the driveway to the other and said, "Let it go, let it go." He did a work in my life in five seconds that sometimes could not be done in months for others. The Holy Spirit coming and helping me to let go of missing the depth of Dorothy's love was a sovereign act of God. Not everyone, in fact not too many at all, have this type of experience. I went from knowing that I had no one to unpack things with anymore to knowing that I was whole and complete as a single person in a matter of five seconds by a supernatural touch. I still missed Dorothy but missing the depth of her love was something that I had let go of and the Holy Spirit took care of me.

My neighbour did not have the luxury of this experience, an encounter with the Holy Spirit, and she basically said, "I have lost my husband through no fault of my own and if God brings someone along that can help me I am going to take the opportunity." I understood where she was coming from and I also understood the pressure that she was having put on her by others. It's amazing how people can go through a relationship break up and divorce and meet someone else soon after and no one really thinks twice about it, but if a person loses a loved one through death how could they even think of seeing someone else? I know for me to have friendships with single women and married women before Dorothy died was fine but afterwards some of these friendships were questioned because I was now single and that made life very difficult for me to navigate through.

As a result of my experience I knew what my neighbour was going through. Some people, in order to cope with the void that is now there because they have lost a loved one enter into a relationship with someone else very quickly. I can honestly say I understand and get why this happens. In my life I hoped to continue on with friendships that I already had but in some cases it became very difficult. It is very easy for people to judge what they think is appropriate and inappropriate but unless they have experienced the death of a spouse for themselves they can, unintentionally, contribute further to the pain and suffering that a person is going through. A person in this position needs love and understanding and people who are willing to listen to them because they have lost their closest friend. It wasn't easy for me going through this nor was it easy for my neighbour, but through it all I was able to offer a listening ear to help her express the anguish in her heart.

After having this conversation with my neighbour I then took my children out to Sofia's (which has now become our favourite family restaurant!), because it was too late to go to church. We had a very interesting conversation which really helped me understand how they were going.

Kelby was very quick to ask what I was talking about to my neighbour and so I proceeded to tell them about the difficulties that this lady was experiencing and how she had formed a friendship with a man she met at a funeral. The children were very quick to give their opinion. Kalani said virtually straight away that it was far too soon to start a friendship with anyone else. Jayden then expressed that if she thought she was ready to move on she should and Kelby basically said as long as they both liked the X-Box it was fine! We all laughed at this and then Kalani offered some further thoughts that she had. She said that she had thought about it a bit more and that if our neighbour was trying to replace her husband then it was wrong, but if she was in a position where she was ready to move on then it was okay.

I was really able to relate to this new insight that Kalani gave and apply it to Dorothy. The moment I start to try and find a replacement for Dorothy things are never going to work out. Dorothy was a unique, beautiful woman and I am never going to be able to replace her and nor do I want to try. The moment you start going down that path it puts unfair pressure on anyone else you begin a friendship with, because they have to live up to the bench mark set by someone else. A person is only ready to be able to move on when they are willing to accept someone else for who they are and not put expectations on them of having to live up to the memories of another.

After this amazing insight from Kalani the children went for it! "What about you dad? What if you find someone else?" were the questions that came out very quickly. After taking the initial onslaught of questions it was very interesting to hear their views.

They were very concerned about me meeting someone and them having an 'evil stepmother'. "You better listen to us dad if she treats us badly behind your back" was one of the concerns they voiced. All the Disney movie stories came out, as well as the Sound of Music scenario where I had better not think about shifting them off to boarding school! The children were more than open about the possibility of my meeting someone else but I had better be prepared to listen to them if they were not being treated right!

In all of this, the conversation was so insightful as to where the children were at and from this has arisen a whole new way of looking at moving on and being open to it. It has not only helped with preparing the hearts and minds of my children and me but also others as well.

The key thing that keeps coming back to me at this time in relation to being single is found in **1 Corinthians 7:7**.

1 Corinthians 7:7 *"But I wish everyone were single, just as I am. But God gives to some the gift of marriage, and to others the gift of singleness." (NLT)*

I know at this time I have been given the gift of singleness and it happened when I experienced the Holy Spirit 'blanketing' me. The gift of singleness to me is recognising that you are whole and complete as a single person and that you are not lacking anything because you are not married. My pursuit of God has become vital to every aspect of my life. In terms of the idea of remarrying, I have found **1 Corinthians 7:35** to be very helpful.

1 Corinthians 7:35 *I am saying this for your benefit, not to place restrictions on you. I want you to do whatever will help you serve the Lord best, with as few distractions as possible. (NLT)*

Prior to this verse Paul had just been speaking about how he wished that everyone were single as he was single but he understood that it wasn't for everyone. I personally have taken the following mindset. I am not closed to the possibility of marrying again but the question that I will ask in relation to anyone I meet is, "Can we serve God better by pursuing Him together than if we were both to remain single?" I believe that if the answer is "Yes" to this question then I would be prepared to remarry.

Ecclesiastes 3:1-4 *To everything there is a season. A time for every person under heaven: A time to be born, And a time to die; A time to plant, And a time to pluck what is planted. A time to kill, And a time to heal; A time to break down, And a time to build up; A time to weep, And a time to laugh. A time to mourn, And a time to dance. (NKJV)*

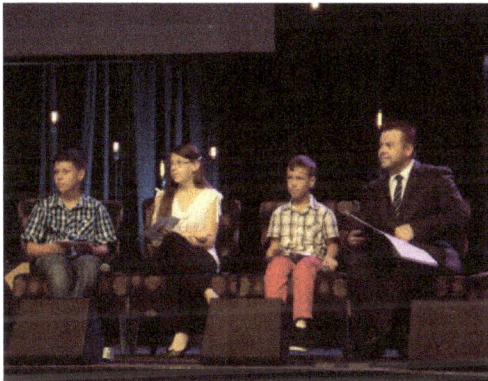

There is a time for everything and for now the time for me is to know God and make God known. Making the most of opportunities that have come my way has not only allowed me to be a blessing to others but also allowed others to be a blessing to me.

Chapter 32: The Year Of Firsts - Dawn Of A New Day

The year of 'firsts' finally came to an end on the 27th of March, 2015 and so ended one of the toughest years of my life but also a year where I could really say that God was able to use the grief we had gone through to shape and fashion us.

In this year of 'firsts', that is, those significant times where Dorothy would have always played a major role, things had generally been going along all right but by far the most difficult thing to deal with was my birthday. This was one of the last things to deal with in the year of 'firsts' some three weeks before the anniversary of Dorothy's death. Handling things like our wedding anniversary, Easter, Dorothy's birthday, Christmas, New Years Eve and the children's birthdays had all been okay as I was still able to make the day special for the children and myself. Even though Dorothy was not there with us we would still remember her and we would have fun together.

The reason my birthday was tougher than any of the other days was because it had always been Dorothy who had made the day special for me and the kids being kids needed her guidance to help make the day special. I had taken the children shopping two nights before my birthday, so they could find something for me. They found plenty of things they liked but didn't look at all for a gift for me! It brought to light just how important Dorothy's touch was and I didn't know what to do. I ended up having a small chat with the children about it and we went shopping again the next night to a golf shop on Kelby's suggestion and this time the children were asking me what I thought about everything! They ended up responding beautifully to my guidance and chose some great presents.

On the day itself they made breakfast for me (bacon and eggs). We had a nice lunch together and then we went to see a movie together (Paper Planes). In hindsight it was probably not the best choice of movie for me. I had been told to be careful with it by a friend at work but I thought the children and I could handle it. I was partially right. The children handled it well and I cried a lot! The reason being is that the background plot to the movie is based around the boy's father who has lost his wife five months earlier due to a car accident and he was not coping well at all and spent a lot of time in despair, sorrow and sadness, watching old VHS tapes of his wife and son. This of course stirred up a lot of my own memories and I had very wet sleeves, trying to hold it together - I failed miserably!

The children and I had a great chat about it afterwards and laughed a lot and we came to the conclusion it was still well worth seeing. We then had a spit roast for tea with Kalani making the salads and we had a cake which was beautifully provided for me by students in my Year 12 Home Group class the day before. A friend also came around that evening and we watched a movie after a late tea. This time it was a science fiction, action film and I can assure you there were no tears with this one! All in all I ended up having a wonderful day, although I can honestly say that I initially was not looking forward to it at all with Dorothy not being there. However, God was still right there with me and He got me through it.

The final thing to get through was the anniversary of Dorothy's death and I had been thinking a little about how to approach it but unexpected help came from other sources! Two days before the anniversary on Friday the 27th of March, 2015 I had just finished playing a soccer practice match and the club president came up to me and gave me a card. It was a card given on behalf of the club to let me know that the soccer club was thinking of my family and myself in relation to the anniversary of Dorothy's death and there were also some tickets to a Melbourne Victory game inside. It was a really nice gesture and I decided that the children and I would finish the day of the anniversary of her death by going out together to Aami stadium to watch the soccer.

On the day before the anniversary I chose to take the children to Lilydale Memorial Park where we have a plaque for Dorothy. Like the day Dorothy was buried, it was wet with drizzle and we just spent a short time there reflecting upon her life and then we went home and watched a whole series of photos from our around the world trip. It was a special time of remembering the wonderful time that we had together as a family when we travelled together for three months.

It was also significant that on the morning of the day before the anniversary of Dorothy's passing, I received a picture when I woke up at 4.00 am. As I was just lying there I saw myself coming up to two big, massive black doors and just walking up and pushing them open. A little like Aragorn walking through the two big doors in the Lord of the Rings. As I pushed through the big doors I saw before me a whole new horizon. It was extremely bright, like coming out of a long tunnel, and it was as if a whole new world had opened up. The sense of peace and freedom I experienced was profound as I contemplated this picture. The year of 'firsts' was over and it was a new beginning and a new day. God has been with me and the children throughout and I know He will continue to be.

On the morning of the anniversary I arrived at work and found a card on my desk. It was from a Year 12 student in my Home Group who was just letting me know that she was thinking of me and the children. What was an amazing confirmation to me was the verse that she gave me.

Revelation 3:8 *I know your works. Behold I have set before you an open door, which no one is able to shut. I know that you have but little power, and yet you have kept my word and have not denied My name. (NKJV)*

Receiving this verse meant so much to me and to the children and we now face all that lies before us with a sense of hope in our hearts. God is enough for me and He is enough for the children. He has been with us throughout the time of Dorothy's illness, He was intimately with us when Dorothy left this life speaking to her in a powerful way as she breathed her last and He has been with us throughout this last year as we have had to deal with grief.

This is the testimony of a man who resolved in His heart to serve the Lord no matter what the outcome. To know beyond a shadow of a doubt that God has been with us through it all, and will continue to be, has caused us to increase in our spiritual hunger to a level we never knew was possible. I can truly say, "My suffering was good for me, for it taught me to pay attention to Your decrees." (**Psalm 119:71** NLT)

The script didn't go the way I would have written it, but the God I love and serve is in control and He knows His plans and purposes for us, especially in this new horizon that lies before us. It is the dawn of a new day.

May God bless you all no matter what life brings your way!

Contact:

Alistair Pitman can be contacted by email at the following email address if you should wish to ask any questions or would just like to communicate some of your thoughts and experiences in your journey of life: pitofgold@optusnet.com.au

About The Author:

Alistair Pitman lives in Melbourne, Australia. He was raised in a Christian home and made a decision to follow Christ at a very young age. He was baptised in water and had an encounter with the Holy Spirit at the age of fifteen. He completed a Bachelor of Education at Deakin University, and also completed Bible College during this time under the guidance of Kevin Conner and David Searle while attending Waverley Christian Fellowship (now known as Citylife Church Knox). He married his wife Dorothy in 1993 and they did life together, raising their three wonderful children (Kalani, Jayden and Kelby) until the 27th of March, 2014. It was at this point that Dorothy left this life to enter into the joy of the Lord after a long battle with illness.

Alistair still attends Citylife Church Knox, with his three children, which is under the leadership of Senior Minister, Mark Conner. He is currently a teacher at Plenty Valley Christian College in the northern suburbs of Melbourne, working with students between the ages of thirteen to eighteen. He is passionate about inspiring and motivating people to turn to God, encouraging them to enter into greater depths and dimensions in their relationship with Him. As a school teacher he loves to use the curriculum as an avenue to talk about the reality of God. The desire of his heart is to diligently seek God, in order to know Him and make Him known.

The ripples from Dorothy's life have profoundly affected him and set the wheels in motion for him to serve God like never before. His passion and hunger for the things of God is infectious and even though he is now raising three children as a single dad, he knows that God is with Him and helping him every step of the way. God continues to give him the strength to live this life, as well as minister to others and offer hope in the midst of suffering and pain. To this day he still declares, "How could I possibly have gone through what I have without a loving God to help support and guide me?"

www.ingramcontent.com/pod-product-compliance
Lightning Source LLC
Chambersburg PA
CBHW052111090426
42741CB00009B/1769